THE BUSINESS
OF WRITING

Gordon Wells

First published in Great Britain in 1998 by
Allison & Busby
114 New Cavendish Street
London W1M 7FD
http://www.allisonandbusby.ltd.uk

A catalogue record for this book is available from
the British Library.

ISBN 0 7490 0362 6

Designed and typeset by N-J Design Associates
Romsey, Hampshire
Printed and bound in Great Britain by
MPG Books Ltd, Bodmin, Cornwall

CONTENTS

ACKNOWLEDGEMENTS

My sincere thanks go to all my writer friends who responded so readily and helpfully to the questionnaire I inflicted upon them – which responses resulted in the sixteen ProFiles included in this book. Without the ProFiles – and the many other brief comments elsewhere throughout – the book would be of less value.

INTRODUCTION

This book is not like other Writers' Guides. It won't tell you how to write. It assumes you already know how to join your words together. But the writing is *only* the creative part of the process; the rest of the process involves the writer in the world of business. Some writers either don't understand or don't want to be bothered by the non-creative aspects – and they nearly always lose out. This book will suggest how you can and should be ... business-like.

Most established writers won't need a book like this: they are already business-like – or they employ someone to be business-like on their behalf. The writers who need this book are those in the early throes of enthusiasm; those who write in their spare time; those sweating over the pages of their first novel; those for whom writing is still a hobby, ideally a paying hobby.

If that's you – someone for whom writing is a paying hobby, as it was for me until I gave up the day job for a pension – it is particularly important to be business-like. Your writing may be merely your spare-time hobby but you are operating in a full-time world of business. You're probably the only spare-time amateur among a gaggle of wage-earning pros. Unless you *behave* like a pro, you could get taken to the cleaners. And that's what this book is all about – showing how you can act the professional, even if you're not.

If your bread and butter depend on your writing, you have to ensure that the payments keep rolling in. Even more so if you also like jam on the bread. You can't afford the luxury of restricting your output to what you want to do – you've got to keep writing. You may need to diversify.

1

The writing world – books

The writing world is vast and diverse. If you run out of ideas in one area of writing – try doing something else. Not only will this keep you occupied – and cheerful, for an idle writer is usually an unhappy writer – but you may discover an unfulfilled side of yourself. And, with a bit of luck, you will be pulling in the cheques too.

Let's look briefly at the extent of the writing world. It does not merely divide up into fiction and non-fiction, short and long, but those over-wide classifications will get us started.

In my mind, I tend to divide book-length fiction into just two categories: 'literary' (or 'straight'), and 'popular' (or 'genre'). Admittedly, that is too simplistic – but is it very wrong? Not in the first category.

Within my literary category, I think of 'the Great British Novel' – the type of book considered for the Booker and similar literary prizes, the novels that are reviewed in the Sunday broadsheets. Too often, such books are little read. They may be bought, to display on the coffee table, but are seldom 'un-put-down-able' and are often given up after a chapter or so. And many sink without trace. This is the type of writing favoured by teachers of creative writing – writing from within, writing for oneself rather than for the market. It's often un-business-like writing.

Then there are the 'popular' novels – the novels that are read, in vast numbers, in paperback, by 'ordinary' people. These are the novels in the airport and station bookshops, the novels that make money – some of them. Here, the category is over-broad. They are popular novels – but that embraces a wide range of very different genres. Popular genres include romance, 'women's interests', sagas, historicals, crime, thrillers, erotica, science-fiction, fantasy, westerns ... and various sub-genres and combinations of these. There are even books of comic-strip pictures, known as graphic novels – but nowadays, their popularity is limited to a narrow, mainly young male, readership. (And no, the authors of such books don't have to draw the pictures, they merely describe them, and write the dialogue, etc.)

If you are a beginning writer, contemplating your first novel, give serious thought to making it a genre novel rather than a literary one.

ProFile 1

Writer Simon Brett

Biog Simon Brett is the author of over 50 books. Some are crime novels – the Charles Paris and Mrs Pargeter series, as well as *A Shock to the System*, which was filmed starring Michael Caine. Some are humorous, including the best-selling *Little Sod* series. And some are anthologies, like *The Faber Book of Parodies* and *The Faber Book of Diaries*. Simon has also written extensively for the stage, radio and television, notably the long-running series *After Henry*. He has been chairman of the Crime Writers' Association and of The Society of Authors.

Question What are your thoughts on the *practice* of writing?

The best writing flows effortlessly. Being a professional writer involves learning techniques to make what has been bloody hard work, read as if it has flowed effortlessly. In the words of Joseph Joubert, 'A fluent writer always seems more talented than he is. To write well, one needs a natural facility and an acquired difficulty.'

You cannot keep yourself out of a book, and you shouldn't try to. Writing a book is an enormous commitment of time and energy. If you've devoted all that to a project you don't believe in, it will certainly show in your writing. As Dorothy Parker observed, 'If you're going to write, don't pretend to write down. It's going to be the best you can do, and it's the fact that it's the best you can do that kills you.'

There is a basic rule of writing: 'If it's boring you, then it's sure as hell going to bore your readers.'

Nothing you write is wasted. Ideas that do not work in one context can, many years later, fit perfectly into another. Anything you write is worth writing, even if the only thing it teaches you is never to write anything like it again. We all learn by our mistakes, and nobody else can make your mistakes for you. You have to make your own.

A skill that develops through a writer's career is the ability to recognise ideas that have potential. Often you won't know in what direction the potential lies, but you will know 'there's something in that.' Make a note, and one day the perfect development of the idea may come to you.

A first novel fitting clearly within a single, recognisable genre has a much greater chance of being accepted by a publisher than does a literary one.

Still with books, the non-fiction field is far bigger than that of novels. A non-fiction book has from five to ten times more chance of achieving publication in the United Kingdom today than does a novel. A non-fiction book can be anything from a biography or autobiography to a school text-book; from a coffee-table book about flowers, gardens, antiques or design, to a 'How-to' book on almost any activity. Whatever your interest there is always the possibility of writing a non-fiction book about it – if you know enough about the subject.

The writing world – magazines

Think now about shorter pieces of writing, potentially for magazine publication. Again, there is fiction and there is non-fiction.

The opportunities for short commercial fiction are no better than for the novel. Most short stories are published in women's magazines; most – but certainly not all – therefore contain some element of romance in their plots. But this can sometimes be associated with a thriller, crime or ghost element. If you want to write short stories for other than the women's magazines – or the occasional specialised science fiction story – there are very limited opportunities for paid publication. You would need to investigate the possibility of writing for the small press magazines, for little or no payment. And writing for free is not what this book is all about.

The scope for writing non-fiction – feature articles – for magazines is, as with books, far greater than that for fiction. Many more magazines publish occasional freelance-contributed articles than publish short stories; most magazines publish more articles than short stories in any issue. Potentially, you could write and sell an article about anything from antique-collecting to zoology, from an arthritis cure to the love-life of Emile Zola.

There is writing for adults and writing for children – and most of the already outlined openings exist for children's writing as well as for adults'. Short fiction for children too has additional, oft-forgotten opportunities, such as in writing picture-scripts for comics – 'graphic short stories'. (There are occasional overlooked opportunities too for non-fiction and/or educational picture-scripts. I've recently sold several one-page potted picture-biographies to a children's magazine.)

The writing world – other media

It is also too easy to overlook the opportunities for writing for the other-than-paper-based media: fiction and non-fiction, plays and documentaries, for the radio, the television and for the stage. It *is* possible to break into these fields and if you are successful, the rewards can be great.

There are writing opportunities too outside the broad publishing world. Maybe you can write a politician's speech for him; commercial firms often need press notices and publicity brochures; the advertising world has many potential openings for writers. It is worth keeping an eye/ear open for such opportunities. (I've written publicity brochures, but no political speeches ... yet.)

Many writers supplement their – sometimes meagre – writing income by talking. There are one-off talks to writers' circles or schools, or to groups like the WI – there is much interest in 'how writers do it' – and there may be scope for teaching writing, often in evening adult education classes. (There's more about lecturing in Chapter 8.)

Try something new

The purpose of the above brief overview of the writing world is to illustrate the diversity of the opportunities for the business-like writer. It is worth giving consideration to all areas of the world: maybe you can extend your activities; maybe you are struggling unsuccessfully merely because you are in the wrong area for you.

Think carefully about your writing objectives or ambitions. These might be:

- to 'get into print' – anything, anywhere (books or magazines, fiction or non-fiction);
- to become a 'respected' – well-reviewed – novelist;
- to make money – 'a living', even – from your writing;
- to be a published author – of either fiction or non-fiction.

Your objective/ambition may influence your choice of writing field in which to work. It should not affect the business-like attitude with which you approach your writing.

For many years I wrote solely non-fiction – first articles and later, when I'd learnt my trade, books. I didn't think I had the necessary imagination to write fiction. (I was also put off by the need to complete a whole novel before discovering whether it would sell: with non-fiction books, the author sells the idea before the book is written.) Then, encouraged by friends, I had a go at fiction. My first book, a romance, was significantly awful – but I had established that I had an imagination capable of dreaming up a fiction plot. Since then, I've written a good number of children's stories – in both straight text and picture-script. Nowadays, if I run out of ideas for one area of my writing activities I can usually come up with an idea in another area. I've diversified – and it's paid off. I'm still a non-fiction writer, but I've proved to myself that I can do other things too.

Market research

Whatever your writing field – fiction or non-fiction, long or short – one thing separates the business-like professional from the beginning wannabe. That one thing is research. Not just subject research, which is seldom overlooked even by the beginner, but market research.

No sensible, business-like professional would dream of writing in total isolation, without thought of what to do with the end product. The professional knows – at least broadly but more likely

6

specifically – which magazine or publisher will be interested in what he or she is writing. The business-like writer knows the market for their work – or has an agent who looks after this side of things on the client's behalf.

How can a wannabe writer acquire the necessary knowledge of the magazine and book-publishing market-place?

First, for both UK magazines and book-publishers, there are the standard reference handbooks:

- *The Writers' & Artists' Yearbook*, published annually by A & C Black;
- *The Writer's Handbook*, published annually by Macmillan/PEN.

These can usefully be supplemented by my own much more detailed, but selectively-limited scope, handbooks:

- *The Magazine Writer's Handbook*, published biennially by Allison & Busby; and
- *The Book Writer's Handbook*, published ever few years by Allison & Busby.

For information on book publishers, there are few more useful reference books than the two special, Spring and Autumn Books, bumper issues of *The Bookseller*. *The Bookseller* is the weekly magazine of the bookselling trade: twice a year they publish special issues listing and categorising all the books which publishers tell them they expect to publish in the next six months; in the same inch-thick issues, many publishers also advertise these same forthcoming books. The two bumper issues are an excellent way of determining the type of books each publisher is (or was – it's a rapidly changing world) likely to be interested in. Authors can subscribe to just the two special issues of *The Bookseller* – or they can almost certainly be found in the reference section of your local public library.

(To subscribe to *The Bookseller* special issues, contact J Whitaker & Sons, 12 Dyott Street, London WC1A 1DF. Tel: 0171-420 6080. Cost is about £40 per year, just for the two issues.)

All such reference books are out of date by the time they reach the bookshop/library shelves. Various small writing magazines and

---

ProFile 2

Writer Jacqueline Wilson

Biog Previously, wrote crime novels for adults and numerous short stories for magazines, but for the past 15 years has happily concentrated on writing for children – over 50 children's books to date.

Credits include the Children's Book of the Year Award in 1993 with *The Suitcase Kid* – and again in 1996 with *Double Act*, which also won the Smarties Prize. *The Bed and Breakfast Star* won the *Telegraph* Book of the Year Award in 1995 – and she has been short-listed for the Carnegie Medal four times.

Question As a children's writer, how do you handle their requests for advice for beginner-writers?

I get lots and lots of letters from 8 to 12 year olds asking for advice and writing tips. I reply to them all and generally suggest they just write for fun. (There's plenty of time to take it seriously and study the market when they're grown up.) I also suggest keeping a diary as good writing practice but I recommend hiding it if they confide too many incriminating secrets!

---

newsletters offer up-dating information but even so, there is still need for closer, more detailed, personal study.

Detailed market study – magazines

Starting with magazines, the wannabe writer should buy two or three up-to-date issues of a small number of target magazines. Two or three copies because you can't identify regular writers for example, from a single copy; up-to-date issues because magazines change their attitudes and slants as often as they change editorial staff; and a small number of target magazines because you can't expect to know all there is to be known about a large number of targets.

INTRODUCTION

One of the first tasks in the market study of a magazine is to ascertain its typical readership. The typical reader is the person you, the writer, will be aiming your work at.

With each issue, start by looking at the advertisements. Producers employ advertising agencies to – among other things – place the advertisements for their products where they will be seen by the greatest number of potential customers. When studying a potential market, a writer can work back from the advertisements to the customer – the typical reader. Of course, the writer will not be able – nor need – to be as precise as the advertising agency. But advertisements for stair lifts, for example, suggest a somewhat elderly, relatively affluent readership. Advertisements for tinned spaghetti hoops and ready-mixed cake ingredients might suggest a slightly down-market reader with small (-ish) children. Study *all* the advertisements and you will gradually build up a picture of the average reader and their interests. Once the readership is identified, you can write material that will interest them – and have more chance of it being accepted.

But magazine market research cannot be restricted merely to the advertisements. Whether you write fiction or non-fiction, read the short stories and serials in the sample magazines; note the ages, genders, interests and activities of the main characters – these will usually reflect those of the readership. Read the articles and note the subjects and how they are treated – is the magazine broad-minded and brash, or cautiously conventional? This is what the magazine wants; this is what you must supply.

Accurately assess the lengths of stories and articles. Count the words. These will be the lengths the magazine wants and the lengths to which you must tailor your work. An editor will not, unless desperate, trim back over-wordy material to the length required nor add material to under-length submissions. Note the writing style of the stories and articles too: are they written in an easy-to-read, tabloid style or a heavy, more literary style? Again – go thou and do likewise.

The editor of a magazine wants to buy material that *fits*; the editor will not adjust the magazine's requirements to accommodate what you deign to offer. It's a buyer's market.

Detailed market study – books

In some ways, the study of publishers' requirements and preferences is more difficult than studying a magazine. Books can vary in many ways – length, treatment, approach, etc. – and what is unacceptable to one publisher may be ideal for another. These are matters which the wannabe author must try to ascertain.

The first step in studying the market for a book is – from the reference books listed above, and from looking at library and bookshop shelves – to make a short list (half a dozen, say) of potential, *relevant* publishers. Contact the chosen few – phone them – and request a copy of their current catalogue. Study it carefully: has the *slant* of the list changed since you assessed it in the reference books? Are you sure the book you want to write will fit this publisher's list? (It is amazing how many potentially worthwhile books, are offered to totally unsuitable publishers: romances to non-fiction publishers, and vice versa, 'How-to' books to publishers specialising in literary biographies.)

Beg, borrow or buy copies of at least two or three of a potential publisher's books of a similar nature to the one you are proposing to write. Determine the preferred length of similar novels, look at the content – the way the book is written. (One publisher's romance list may contain little explicit sex, another's, a lot. And many romance publishers have specific length requirements.)

If your book is to be non-fiction, search diligently for a series into which it might be tailored to fit. Books usually sell better in series than as one-offs ... and therefore have a better chance of being commissioned. If you find a potentially joinable series, make a detailed study of how one of that series' books is put together. But if there is no suitable series, don't despair: lots of non-fiction books do sell as one-offs. (An encouraging anecdote: I found a one-off book along the same lines as one I hoped to write. I persuaded the publisher that mine would sit comfortably alongside the existing one ... and that was the start of the flourishing Allison & Busby Writers' Guides series. Dianne Doubtfire's *The Craft of Novel-Writing* was book one, my *Craft of Writing Articles* was book two. Both are still in print well over a dozen years later.)

Learning to write

Having said, at the start, that this book is for those who already know how to join words together, some professionally-minded as-yet-wannabe writers may feel the need for greater expertise. There is no doubt that many of the *techniques* – characterisation, writing dialogue, preparing synopses, etc. and presentation (see also Chapter 5 in this book) – of the writing business can be taught and learned. I also believe that, given some specialist knowledge – and the willingness to work very hard – almost anyone can learn to write competent non-fiction. (See also Appendix 3.)

What is less certain is whether the ability to tell a story can be taught and learned. And it is fiction that most wannabes wannawrite.

Writing cannot be taught. A person has to want to write and have an aptitude for writing. But, if they've got those two things, listening to the advice of more experienced writers can save them an awful lot of time.

Simon Brett

Whatever your writing interest, you will also be stimulated and encouraged by any of the writing guides that are on the bookshelves. The writers who give you a personal insight into your preferred genre, are professional people who have learned by their own successes and failures, who know all about rejections and all the other highs and lows of a writing life. Whatever you want to write, there's a book out there that will guide you on your way. It won't teach you talent, because that is something within you, but it will certainly stop you falling into the many pitfalls and traps that prevent your way to publication.

Jean Saunders

No one can learn to be a writer. You need all sorts of qualities – the ability to tell a story, empathy with other people, originality of thought – but few of them can be taught. I run writers' workshops myself, and believe the most important thing I can do, apart from demonstrating a few practical things, is to stimulate and excite the up-coming writers who attend my classes sufficiently to make them want to rush home and start working on their books.

Susan Moody

The techniques of working on your writing can be learned from the many 'How-to' books currently on the market. (Inevitably, I believe that the books in the Allison & Busby Writers' Guides series, for which I am the editorial adviser, are the most useful. But many others are good too.)

Both correspondence courses in writing and creative writing evening classes are also ideal for learning the techniques. Their ability to bring out nascent talent however is less certain: much will depend on the writing experience and teaching skills of the individual tutors. The better tutors acknowledge that the most they can hope to do – beyond teaching technique – is to excite and inspire the students to go and do their own thing(s).

Writers' circles are like curate's eggs – some are good, some are not so good. Many writers' circles concentrate on helpful mutual criticism – which can result in the blind leading the blind. Before you get too enthusiastic about the undoubted delights of the company of like-minded writers, consider the basis, relevance, expertise, and value of their always well-meaning criticisms. Find out just whose criticisms are worth taking note of – and whose to ignore gracefully.

Academic qualifications

Beyond the above, basically everyday, opportunities to learn the techniques of writing, it is fast becoming *the thing* for universities up and down the land to offer MA courses in creative writing.

The University of East Anglia was among the first to offer such a course – with leading authors as tutors. Although I believe that storytelling is a talent with which one has to be born, the UEA course has certainly succeeded in fostering several new writers. The right encouragement – and the opportunity/pressure – to produce one's best work, undoubtedly works there. But one wonders what the course adds, apart from that.

I suspect that a degree in creative writing would be of considerable value if you already have the basic raw talent and that certain imaginative spark. Presumably such a course would teach you how to develop characters, how to escalate suspense, how to use viewpoint for effect, how to pace your story and how to write convincing dialogue. In other words, you can learn to improve your writing by the clever use of writing techniques, but you cannot be taught that basic gift of *storytelling*.

However, not having a degree need not deter anyone who can write. You can teach yourself if you have the right commitment. If your grammar is weak, buy a suitable book or attend evening classes. (Don't expect an editor to correct your grammar for you.) Attend workshops, read books on structure and characterisation, study films and analyse them. Read good fiction as well. You will subconsciously absorb much that is useful.

And, of course, it helps to recognise your weaknesses. If you don't know them, how can you work to eradicate them? And learn to accept criticism – but only from those who know. Well meaning friends and relatives may offer conflicting advice and will confuse you. Better to ask for help from experienced and successful writers and/or tutors. A good editor is invaluable.

Pamela Oldfield

Academic qualifications are only of value to a writer to impress the natives. A good degree in a relevant subject from a quality university can open doors (mine has) but beware spurious qualifications from doubtful sources. Of course, in themselves, qualifications don't make anyone a good writer. What *can* be taught to a writer? They could buy one of my books and find out ... [Didn't I say that a business-like writer had to be a tad pushy? GW.]

Jill Dick

Attitude

The wannabe writer needs more than encouragement though. The wannabe writer has to develop an *attitude*, a *will to succeed* – and a professional approach. The professional *attitude* comes across well in the many helpful comments in Appendix 3.

ProFile 3

Writer Diana Pullein-Thompson

Biog Diana Pullein-Thompson comes from a family of writers. She and her sisters, Josephine and Christine, are remembered by generations of children for their 'pony' books – which began in 1946 with *It Began with Picotee*. Many of Diana's children's books have been widely translated. Writing as Diana Farr, she has written two biographical works. She has also contributed to the American *Dictionary of Literary Biography* and OUP's *New Dictionary of National Biography*.

Credits include children's books, *Cassidy in Danger*, *The Long Ride Home*, and *Ponies in Peril*; adult books include *Choosing* (a novel) and *A Georgian Prodigy*, the standard biography of Gilbert Cannan.

Question Do you think that academic qualifications (e.g. an MA in Creative Writing) are of any relevance to a writer's chances of success?

I can't generalise; too much depends on the course and the tutors. Authors are individuals with individual needs and aspirations. Several have clearly benefited from reading for an MA in creative writing, but the insight, imagination and curiosity which drives most authors to write fiction cannot be taught; the way to handle material, to dramatise events and add pace to a story can. Certainly, the eye of a kindly and expert tutor on a would-be-writer's story can work wonders, but too much consequent self-assessment may inhibit inspiration. Short writing courses are undoubtedly stimulating for isolated and lonely authors, but a true writer will probably keep on writing as long as he or she can wield a pen or sit at a typewriter or computer. An MA may raise intellectual achievement and help serious authors to receive a grant and if offered a place at, for example, UEA, I would advise an author to take it. But, in the end, what matters most is talent, stoicism and the ability to survive the ups and downs of authorship

INTRODUCTION

The wannabe writer has to believe that he or she WILL succeed. Given that belief, if strong enough, together with a dedication – which boils down to a willingness to work long and hard – the wannabe will succeed.

Being business-like

So, we have looked at the diverse nature of the writing business and how to study the market. If you are not totally happy in your current writing field – or even if you just have some spare time – consider trying something new. The business-like writer needs to keep busy, keep selling, keep writing – and you can only do that if you are enjoying yourself.

Most writers though, once they have cleared the hurdles of their first few acceptances, seem to understand the benefits of diversification and market research. But being business-like is more than that. It's also about using your writing time efficiently and using the right equipment; it's about selling your work – and yourself – in the most effective way; it's about keeping tags on your output ... and on how much money you're making; it's about understanding contracts – safeguarding your rights. And those are the matters that we look at in the rest of this book.

1

MAKING THE MOST OF YOUR TIME

Time is the one thing a busy writer never has enough of. (Except when 'between jobs' and wondering what on earth to write next or why a favourite editor or publisher hasn't yet responded to the latest idea. Yes, it happens to many of us.) Just as in all those 'how to be an efficient manager' articles and the advertisements for loose-leaf organisers, the business-like writer can benefit from organising his/her time.

Regular habits

Whether you write for just an hour a day after 'work' or spend all of every day at it, it pays to be regular. Your 'writing muscle' needs regular exercise. There is a school of thought too, that suggests that, to work at its best, a writer's subconscious needs awakening at the same time each day.

For the beginning, spare-time writer the allotted time may only be short; no matter. The important thing is its regularity. You are getting your brain used to the idea of thinking 'writing' at the same time every day.

There are other benefits which derive from a regular writing time-slot though. The most important is perhaps that it becomes recognised – by immediate family and drop-in friends alike – that from, say, 8.00 to 9.00 pm every day, you are writing, and not to be disturbed. It becomes your 'special time'. Equally, if you work a full 9 to 5 day at your writing, it has to be recognised that you are 'at work' – just as though you were out, at the office.

I have two work patterns. [Stella works several long days each week in the House of Commons.] When the House is sitting and I travel to London, I write on the train, like Trollope, with a pad or draft manuscript on my knee. In the evening this work is then transferred to disk. During the Recesses, I write at my dining-table-desk all morning, take the afternoon off to shop, go to an exercise club, walk or swim, then work again all evening. If it's sunny and the manuscript is in draft, I will work in the garden. Can't waste sunshine.

I am never 'between books'. There's always another one on the way. I often juggle several – at different stages – at the same time. If I have a deadline to meet, then of course that book has my full attention.

I frequently gaze out of the window, day-dream, talk to the cats, cha-cha-cha round the kitchen, sing Gershwin, read endless newspapers and magazines – and books that I've borrowed or bought. But of course, behind all this apparent 'doing nothing', my brain is still working, storing away facts, ideas, and snatches of dialogue.

Stella Whitelaw

Output targets

For some, allotting a regular time-slot is not enough. Many writers give themselves an output target – so many words per day. I firmly believe in this approach – as long as the target does not become a strait-jacket. If you have to struggle with your writing, squeezing out every carefully-chosen word like beads of perspiration, then you need a small target. If the words (usually) flow easily, a larger target is best. Set yourself an achievable target; not one that will cause you stress. You'll feel good when you hit the target day after day. And there's nothing to stop you writing more than your target figure. Remember too, you have only yourself to explain to, when you don't achieve it.

ProFile 4

Writer Jean Saunders (also writes as Jean Innes, Rowena Summers and Sally Blake).

Biog Has written more than 75 novels (including contemporary romances, family sagas, raunchy historicals and erotica), about 600 published short stories, numerous articles and five 'How-to' books (for Allison & Busby). Frequent conference speaker. Past short story columnist for *Writing Magazine*. Past chairman Romantic Novelists Association; past chairman Southern Writers' Conference.

Credits include as Jean Saunders, *The Bannister Girls* (Harper-Collins) – runner-up for Romantic Novel of Year 1991; as Rowena Summers, a quartet of family sagas – *Killigrew Clay*, *Clay Country*, *Family Ties* and *Family Shadows*. Currently writing for Robinson's Scarlet imprint (UK) and Zebra Books (USA) – among others.

Question Do you work regular office hours? When 'between books', do you ever 'do nothing' in a writing sense?

I work office hours, from around 9.00 to 4.30, with at least an hour's break in the middle of the day. It's always been important to me to regard writing as a professional business, and to keep up a steady output, which I believe keeps the mind fresh and stimulated. This was not always possible in the beginning, when I had small children to contend with, but life gets easier. In those days I wrote at the kitchen table, between the obligatory school runs, etc., and my output was limited to short stories, articles and poems.

I have every sympathy for those people who want to write, but lead busy 'other lives' as well. It was only when I was able to devote more time to writing that I began writing novels. Now my office is a converted bedroom, and I am rarely 'between books'. Before I finish one, I'm always thinking about or planning the next, and I sometimes have several on the go at the same time.

I never 'do nothing' in a writing sense. I have rarely had any kind of 'writer's block', and if it threatens I think there are many ways to combat it. The way I find most helpful is to keep involved in some way other than actually writing. For me, this means that if I'm not physically working on a novel or a How-to article, I may be researching or checking facts, answering mail or the telephone – or questionnaires – or planning courses or conference notes. It's all involved with the world of writing which I love.

Time has always been a problem for me. Finding it, keeping it, using it well, and not getting exhausted by it. I work five days a week managing a busy city centre store and this does not constitute the easy life that many imagine. It is a pressured job: negotiating the right deal, fulfilling supply contracts, hitting targets, getting plagued by authors who all want to know why their title isn't in the window. And then complained at by customers who always want to buy the books you've never heard of, or just sent back. It is not an atmosphere to write in – although having so much reference material close to hand can often help.

To write I require uninterrupted peace, half an hour here and an hour there will not do it. I need a stretch of time and preferably preceded by a period of winding down. People who are not writers find this hard to understand. I do my shop work Tuesday to Saturday, spend Sunday mowing the lawn or with the family and then devote Monday to creative work. Over the years I have learned to be disciplined. I rise early, move seamlessly to the study, turn on both the PC and the music and then go. The phone gets dealt with by BT's excellent Call-minder, the door gets ignored. I talk to no one. I just drink tea and work. Eight hours straight – or ten if the inspiration is hot. And I hate it, too. The only time I've ever found to enjoy is the moment when I have just finished. The work is done and I haven't yet begun doubting it or wondering if I could do it again. A bit Zen really but for me that's the only part of the writing process that's worth having. Stay in the moment – don't look back to how long it took or forward to its possible publication. Just enjoy it for what it is. Writing, done.

Peter Finch

When I was a wage-slave, commuting daily to London and writing for just one hour after dinner every night, I set myself a daily target of only 400 words. (I wrote longer hours over the weekend and managed to produce a full book chapter – around 4 to 5,000 words – every ten or twelve days.) Nowadays, with a pension to back me up, I'm a full-time writer. My target is now 800 words a day of whatever book I'm working on (there's usually one on the go), plus various other writing jobs that have to be done, book or no. Almost invariably, I exceed my 800-word target – but I'm not raising it. I enjoy the feel-good factor.

> I try to clear a thousand words a day when I'm working on a book. I don't always succeed, but I try not to give up until I've spent at least half a day on it. Sometimes when it's going well I write more. I usually write for about three hours in the morning and then maybe another couple of hours in the evening. Between books I tend to take a month or six-week break.
>
> Jo Bannister

When comparing my target figures with those of some prolific novelists, remember all the research, planning, organising, selling, etc., that also needs to be done to produce a non-fiction book. I have regular magazine columns to write too, as well as one-off articles. And my writing correspondence file grows inexorably these days.

Recording your output

You can make the most of the aforementioned feel-good factor by keeping a (written) record of your output achievements. If you are in the throes of a book – fiction or non-fiction – a chapter-by-chapter 'word budget' and a daily output wordage will let you keep score. If you are writing shorter material, you could probably just note the daily output figure in your diary. (You DO keep a writing diary, don't you?)

A word budget can be as simple or as complex as you wish.

If you are writing a novel, you have some idea of the overall target length and number of chapters. For a 20-chapter, 100,000-word novel, the word budget need be no more than a chapter-list from 1 to 20, with a target length for each chapter of, say, 5,000 words.

As you complete each chapter compare the achieved length with the 'budgeted' target figure. If you are *consistently* under or over length, the word budget will draw this to your attention. Maybe the finished novel isn't going to be long enough – perhaps you can add in a sub-plot. Maybe you are writing too much material – perhaps you can tighten up your descriptive passages. Or maybe you're going to end up with more or fewer chapters of different lengths. It matters not how you achieve the desired result – the finished, 100,000-word book – only that you are made aware of the need to think about possible adjustments.

If your book is non-fiction, you will be working from a detailed chapter-by-chapter synopsis – on the basis of which you were commissioned to write the book – and an agreed overall length. Your chapters may not be intended to be of equal lengths, but you will have a good idea of how long each ought to be. Your non-fiction word budget will need to compare achieved wordage with more specific chapter target-lengths. You must also remember to allow for 'off-line' material – case studies, illustrations, appendices, etc. – when assessing the overall book length.

In addition to the word budget, which is actually an aid to the writing itself, you can ensure that you keep basking in the feel-good glow by recording your output daily. I record simply: date, output words, and running total. This record makes it clear when I've finished half the book, three-quarters, etc. I can usually find some sort of excuse to celebrate a progress milestone. (Not mere flippancy, that. It is a good idea to give yourself frequent small milestones to celebrate; writing is a lonely business and any encouragement helps. And you can carry this idea a little further: tell yourself that you won't break off for mid-morning coffee until you've written the first 100 words, or reached the chapter-end, or some other self-determined target.)

Avoiding staleness

Seldom a problem with the spare-time writer, snatching the regular daily hour, staleness can become a problem for the 9-to-5 writer. You are working away, against a deadline, writing steadily. The words keep coming, because you've trained yourself to ensure that they do, but somehow ... you know they aren't quite as bright as you would like them to be. You're in a bit of a rut.

There's a cure. Nine times out of ten, you don't output words solidly from 9 to 5, and seldom on one project alone. Most of us have loads of other writing-related tasks to do every day. Maybe you deal with the writing correspondence, or reply to phone calls at the start or the end of each working day. Change your routine. Write the creative stuff for an hour or so, break for coffee, then answer a couple of routine letters or phone calls. Or start the research or planning work on next week's column. After an hour, go back to the 'real' writing. The change will have been ... as good as a rest. The sparkle will be back.

Try it. It works.

Contacts

A further way of making the best use of your writing time is to organise your contacts. Every writer needs contacts – experts on this subject or another, who can give them a quick explanation of something that is holding up the writing process. (Yes, fiction writers need contacts too; it's just as important that the background facts in your story are correct as it is for those in my articles and non-fiction books.)

First though, you have to have the contacts. Start with the obvious. Most of us have at least some friends. And most people are knowledgeable about something. Go through a list of your friends, making a note of who is knowledgeable about what. (Even knowing which of your friends has the biggest address book is useful ... when you need to know where to contact someone.) Extend your coverage: think about acquaintances, people you know/knew at work, and their specialities. Make a note: name and address and special subject.

Now repeat the list but in reverse: subjects first, name and address last. And sort the list out into alphabetical order. Great – you're beginning to establish your ORGANISED list of contacts. When you next want – as I did recently – to insert a snippet of German dialogue into a story, you'll quickly be able to find a note of just who it was who spoke fluent German. (Even schoolboy German would have sufficed for me – I learnt French.)

But existing friends and acquaintances are not sufficient for a business-like writer's list of contacts. It needs to be extended. For that, you need time. Time to build up your list. Whenever you meet someone, make a note of their specialist knowledge. Whenever you consult a contact, ask for the name of any other, perhaps more specialised expert – begin to establish a 'chain of expertise' – and add them to your list.

A useful source of 'standard' contacts are the publications of Carrick Media, Galt House, 31 Bank Street, Irvine, KA12 0LL (Tel: 01294 311322) – the annual *Media Yearbook* and the more frequent *Journalist's Handbook* – which contain lists of useful organisations and their press officers. If you can establish some sort of 'journalist credentials', Carrick Media will happily put you on their mailing list. I've often found their lists useful.

Space to write in

Organising your writing time is one thing, organising your writing space is another. Anthony Trollope – a spare-time author with a day job in the Post Office – who travelled a lot by train in connection with his job, made himself a 'little tablet' on which he wrote, in pencil, on his lap, while travelling. (He turned out a regular 250 words per quarter-hour – and, as recommended above, kept a daily record of his prolific writing output.) Ernest Hemingway is said to have preferred to write standing up. One author apparently wrote on the mantelpiece, standing up, with children milling around underfoot. Most of us, though, need to sit down, with our papers around us. And the more we can organise our writing space to meet our needs, the more relaxed and ready to work we'll be.

> The dining-room table has been commandeered as the writing HQ; the (essential) computer is on another table, and projects on the go are on a third table, the three arranged in a U shape. There is another work area for admin – older files, etc. – on the other side of the room. If I ever get more space I'll have one of those big, book-lined libraries I've gawped at in local National Trust properties.
>
> John Dawes

ProFile 5

Writer Stella Whitelaw

Biog Began her writing life as a cub reporter, eventually becoming the youngest female chief reporter in London. Short stories were her first love until a kindly Scottish editor pointed out that a book or serial is only a string of short stories joined together. Currently, Stella writes cat fiction, true cat stories, romance, longer mystery and suspense, and more recently, crime. Her tally to date: 30 published books and 211 short stories – and she's lost count of foreign sales.

Credits include *Stella Whitelaw's Treasury of Cat Tales* (Mildmay), *The Owl and the Pussycats* (HarperCollins), *Dragon Lady* (Mills & Boon) about cervical cancer screening, *No Darker Heaven* (Scarlet-Robinson) and *How To Write Short-Short Stories* (Allison & Busby).

Question Do you have a special place in which to write? If you could change it, how would you?

For many years I was a kitchen-table writer but the disadvantage of having to clear away every day drove me upstairs to a tiny spare room. It didn't work. I felt too cut off from the children, coffee and an elderly mother.

Then I commandeered the big oval dining table and no one has ever seen its polished top since. It has two word processors on it – my trusty Amstrad PCW 8256 and my wonderful new Wordsmith with its vast memory.

Despite having a custom-built wall of shelves alongside me for research, books, manuscripts and work files, the piles on the floor grow around my feet like mushrooms. There is never any time for filing. Periodically the heaps fall over or get knocked flying by marauding cats. I then have to get down on my knees to do some filing or the carpet cannot be vacuumed.

Amid all the chaos of my corner of the room (idyllic view of garden, Japanese maple and birds feeding), there is an element of organisation. Each project is housed in a fat file, basket tray or box file. But since I am usually working on several books, short stories and ideas at the same time, this degree of order is scarcely visible.

I dream of having a whole study to myself, lined with shelves, orderly, a place for everything, room to move. And a part-time secretary to do the boring clerical work vaguely elsewhere. But I know it wouldn't work. Daughter would gravitate with cups of tea, son fold himself over a chair to chat, several cats would slink in ... one to sit on my lap, one to sprawl on work in progress, a third to install himself in the top letter tray like a managerial paperweight.

No matter how small or temporary your writing work-space, it is important that it is YOURS. Your writing must be sacrosanct. You must know that when you put things away one day, they will be there, unmolested, the next day.

The minimum work-space for a writer is, I suppose, the corner of a table. If that is all you can arrange, you also need a box in which all your work and materials can be safely stored when you are not working. As your writing becomes more and more important though, so you will need more equipment, more reference material, more files. (More on a writer's equipment in the next chapter.) You need a permanent space to which you alone have access.

If it's all you've got, even the cupboard space under the staircase can be converted into a workable study for a writer. Remove the cupboard doors – replace them with a curtain – and open up the whole space. Fix the widest- and longest-possible shelf at table level – propping it, if necessary, to support the near-essential computer (*see* Chapter 2) – and as many more ordinary-sized shelves as possible above it. Seek out one or more two-drawer filing cabinets – ideally on castors – that will fit beneath the table-shelf. Fix a movable-arm desk light to the wall, and maybe a telephone extension socket. Buy an inexpensive office chair, on castors, that will tuck away under the table-shelf; you can sit in the passageway while you're working – the family can squeeze past if they have to. Be sure that when not in use though, everything goes away, unobtrusively, behind the curtain. And make sure that everyone understands that this is YOUR space – out of bounds to everyone else.

Another alternative is what used to be called a 'mini-office' – a cupboard-like piece of furniture which, open, can afford a reasonable work-space plus some filing and shelf-space; yet which, closed, looks like a well-finished side-board or wardrobe. Several furniture manufacturers offer such cupboards – but they are not cheap. (A good one can cost a couple of thousand pounds.)

A room of your own

Maybe you already have a small study – or spare bedroom. Many would consider this an ideal situation. If the bedroom is not 100 per cent 'spare' though, you could lose the use of it when you have visitors – and remember what we have already said about putting in a daily stint of writing. Similarly with a study: you might be expected to 'share' – which could be difficult. Writing is an anti-social habit: like the early film-star Greta Garbo, you need to be alone.

For those who can achieve the luxury of a personal – dedicated – study, from my own personal experience, a wee word of warning. A writer can never have too many bookshelves – your collection always grows to fill the space available. Never fit fixed shelves: opt for the screwed-to-the-wall slotted metal uprights (by Spur, from DIY stores) into which movable shelf-supports can be fitted.

Similarly with files. Buy full-sized filing cabinets – you'll always fill them. To over-flowing. Go for a big desk too: mine's 135 cm x 75 cm ... but the clear worktop space seldom exceeds 70 x 50. And that's with my computer and printer on a separate mobile work station

Some writers – most famously, the late great children's author, Roald Dahl – work in a garden shed. Seemingly, Dahl had to wrap himself in blankets to keep warm. That must always be a problem with ordinary garden sheds. Not for me, thanks. Other writers rent a small office away from home distractions. (If, as a full-time writer, you 'go off to work' like everyone else, and stay away from home during normal office hours, your writing will be taken more seriously – as a 'proper job' – by your peers.) But rented offices cost more than most writers can readily afford.

Finally, if an elderly aunt leaves you an unexpected windfall – of a few thousand pounds – there is a recently launched alternative. A purpose-built, fully fitted (and heated and insulated) octagonal-shaped prefabricated 'garden studio' building, ready-supplied with integral desks, shelving, telephone sockets, lighting, security alarms, etc. offering working space for two tidy people or one untidy writer. Delivered, erected, connected up and ready to use for about the cost of a small new car. It LOOKS really good. Interested – and feeling affluent? Phone Garden Offices Ltd in Croydon on 0181-689 1941.

Profile 6

Writer Susan Moody

Biog Susan Moody was born and educated in Oxford. She lived for some years in France and then in America before returning to England, and Oxford. Her first novel, not crime, was published in America in 1981, under a pseudonym. She began writing crime in 1984 and has been a professional writer ever since. She started with the *Penny Wanawake* crime series, then moved on to the *Cassandra Swann* crime series. Susan has also written five suspense novels and *Misselthwaite*, a sequel to *The Secret Garden*. Past Chairman of the Crime Writers' Association; British Chairman of the International Association of Crime Writers.

Credits include other than those named above, the suspense novels *The Italian Garden* and *Falling Angel* and – under a pseudonym – the best-selling story of the Gold Blend coffee couple, *Love Over Gold*.

Question Do you work regular office hours? When 'between books', do you ever 'do nothing' in a writing sense? Where do you work?

Now that my children have left home, I no longer have to work during their school hours, i.e. between 9.30 and 3.30. However, I try to write regularly and am usually at my desk around 8.30 to 9.00 and stay there, with breaks, until 4.30 or so.

I don't think I'm ever 'between books', in the sense that there is no deadline to meet. All my books are commissioned or contracted.

Doing nothing? Now there's an interesting question. Can a writer of fiction ever be said to be doing nothing 'in a writing sense'? I do find there are days, sometimes a whole string of them, when I don't actually put words to paper. I used to worry about this, or feel guilty, but have learned over time that these days are as important as the ones when I write. There is never a time when I'm not thinking very hard about the current book.

I have my own study (as opposed to one shared with the family), lined with books. An improvement would be a built-in incinerator into which I could dump all the thousands of pieces of paper which demand attention and take up valuable writing time. (I guess that includes such things as my questionnaire: sorry, and thanks, Susan. GW.)

2

TOOLS OF THE TRADE

Once upon a time, all a writer needed was a pen and paper. The very word 'manuscript' implies a hand-written text. But those days are long gone. If you were daft enough to deliver a hand-written text – fiction or non-fiction, magazine- or book-length – to a publisher today, it wouldn't get much attention. (Except perhaps as a freak or museum-piece.) For many years now, anything intended for publication has had to be in typescript.

But the world has moved on even further. The uneven 1950s product of a manual typewriter – complete with 'whited-out' corrections and minor hand-written alterations – would today be looked at askance. It is doubtful whether there is a professional writer left whose work is not now word-processed – either by the writer or by a paid assistant.

(There are still a few famous authors who profess to 'need to feel the words flowing through their body, to the pen, and direct onto the page'. With publishers unwilling to accept hand-written work, one has only to look at the advertisements of those offering to type a writer's work – at several pounds per thousand words – to realise the financial unreality of that attitude for most of us. A business-like writer has to self-type.)

If you don't know how to type – learn. (If young school-leavers can pick it up in a few weeks, surely you can, too?) Once you've learnt, as a writer you'll get plenty of practice.

As yet, there is no major objection to a writer using a typewriter – but preferably not a manual one. Small portable electronic typewriters can now be bought for around a hundred pounds. However, simple-to-use dedicated all-in-one-box word processors cost little more and are infinitely preferable. Think hard before you buy yourself a typewriter ... and then decide on a word processor instead.

Computers

As we have already established, as a writer you are operating in the business world. Those with whom you seek to do business are accustomed to receiving correspondence and other work which LOOKS professional. If you wish to do business, your letters and submissions too must look business-like. (I was recently asked to comment on a book proposal which had been prepared on a manual typewriter. Its content was quite good – but before I could fairly assess it, I had to overcome my instinctive rejection of the awful presentation.)

Looking beyond first experiences with a word processor, most business-like writers will eventually upgrade from the simple self-contained word processor to a full-blooded program-driven computer with a linked but separate printer. There are only two basic choices: any one of a vast number of IBM-compatible personal computers, or one manufactured by Apple. The choice is personal – Apple computers were long favoured for their ease of use but with the latest Microsoft Windows operating systems, any of the IBM-compatible machines (usually referred to as PCs) are pretty well a match for them. Certainly PCs with Microsoft software vastly outnumber Apples in the business world. And because of this, there is vastly more software (the programs that make the computers work in a user-friendly fashion) for the PC than for the Apple.

> I would find it impossible to work without a word processor. It improves and speeds up all the tedious part of producing a manu-script, and leaves more time for the exciting bits, like creating and telling the story.
>
> Susan Moody

But a computer on its own is not a word processor. It needs a printer and a word processor program – to tell it what to do.

Printers

Printers have made huge advances in recent years. And their prices have fallen dramatically, partly because some of their control mechanism has been moved to the computer itself. A laser printer – arguably the best – was for a long time out of the financial reach of most 'ordinary' writers (certainly I couldn't afford one until recently); today a variety of laser printers can be bought for under £300; an ink-jet or 24-pin dot-matrix printer need cost little over £100. (While early 9-pin dot-matrix printers produced 'dotty' typescript that gave computer printing a bad name, the output of 24-pin printers – particularly with a new ribbon – is excellent.)

When considering the purchase of a printer, investigate operating costs as well as just the purchase price. Dot-matrix printers use inexpensive ribbons that wear out gradually as the output fades; laser and ink-jet printer cartridges are much more expensive and just stop when they're empty – but the output is better-looking. You pays yer money ...

Remember though: at the end of the day, editors and publishers won't pay any more for a laser-printed typescript than for a dot-matrix-printed one.

The word processor program

The other essential element of a writer's computer equipment is the word processor program. Without the word processor program, the computer doesn't know how to ... process words.

For many years I used – and raved about – a little-known word processor program called Quill plus a 'typing accelerator' called Jot! Together, they did everything I needed and their use became second nature to me. I still think Quill's a superb program – but it's been overtaken by the advances of other programs, and never updated. It being out-dated didn't much matter to me, until recently.

Increasingly now though, editors and publishers are asking for, or at least welcoming, submissions on disk. (They nearly always want 'hard copy' – i.e., typescript – too.) And while editors and publishers will nearly always accept text in the form of an ASCII file on disk, they may prefer the output from one or other of the most commonly-used word processor programs. (ASCII, appropriately pronounced ass-key, stands for American Standard Code for Information Interchange: virtually all word processors can convert text into ASCII, which can be read direct, as a text file, by any personal computer.) It is therefore an advantage for a writer to use one of the popular programs: Microsoft's Word, Corel's WordPerfect, or Lotus' WordPro. Each has its supporters: Word, being a Microsoft product, is probably the most used/favoured. (I've recently changed allegiance from Quill to Word – which also does much that Jot! did too.)

If you work a lot with one publisher (or one magazine) and are in the throes of changing your word processor program, it is often worth changing to the program used in the publisher's office. Both you and your editor may find this makes life easier – swapping disks, etc.

Other communication equipment

But the computer/word processor is not the only item of essential (or near-essential) equipment for today's business-like writer. A telephone is of course taken for granted: no business-like writer can afford to be out of telephone reach. There are also many profitable, associated, non-writing, activities – giving talks, etc. (see Chapter 8) – which necessitate your being accessible by phone to potential employers.

An answering machine too is important if you are not to miss out on unexpected opportunities. Beware though: answering machines can increase already large phone bills. Responding to an answering machine contact is at your expense, rather than the caller's.

There is no financial disadvantage whatsoever in owning a fax machine though. These are pure advantage. A (professional-looking) fax message reaches the recipient's desk in a flash: it implies urgency and is therefore important; a reply – by scribbled hand-written annotation – can be immediate. A faxed message costs less to send

---

ProFile 7

Writer Jill Dick

Biog Jill Dick has worked on newspapers all her life. She joined the *Sun* at its launch and spent two years as a departmental editor writing and editing a page every day. During this time she also wrote for two Australian dailies under the same management and compiled and edited children's annuals for the *Sun*. For the next 20 years she was children's editor on the *Manchester Evening News*, also working as a theatre critic and feature writer for a wide variety of newspapers and magazines here and overseas. She has wide experience of live theatre at amateur and professional level, is a Classics graduate, a Freeman of the City of London and a thoroughly practical writer.

Credits include *Writing for Magazines* and *Freelance Writing for Newspapers* (both A & C Black, both second editions) ... and *The Directory of Writers' Circles* (now in eighth edition).

Question Are you connected to the Internet? Do you find it useful – and for what?

I have three separate connections. I use it for research – discovering gems intentionally and (of more value) unintentionally that I could surely not find elsewhere. It is an illuminating window on the world that transforms a writer's insight. It is also of unfailing general interest. I would hate to lose the instant communication and invaluable help that e-mail provides.

---

than an ordinary letter and takes less time than a spoken phone call. (I have often had a frantic phone call from an editor or publisher about a lost (short) manuscript or mislaid invoice and resolved the difficulty by the immediate faxing through of a copy. And it certainly speeds up communications when dealing with overseas publishers – the turn-round time for an air mail response can be weeks.)

And from the fax machine it is only a small step to thoughts of electronic mail – e-mail. If you will link your computer, via a modem and telephone socket, to the Internet, you can send material directly and almost instantaneously from your computer screen to that of an editor/publisher.

I'm connected to the Internet, and even have a web-site, though I have a problem accessing it. The only reason I find the Internet useful is for e-mail. What a godsend: it makes corresponding so quick and easy, especially for setting up trips abroad to conferences; I also find that my fellow-writers, relieved of the necessity to find envelopes and stamps, send wonderfully long interesting letters.

Susan Moody

I am not connected to the Internet. I'm happy to do all my corresponding the old-fashioned way. I don't even own a computer.

Jacqueline Wilson

I used to be 'connected' to the Internet, but not now. It was good fun and potentially useful, but there was, and is, too much rubbish for me to weed through or play with by wasting time 'on the browse'. I will return to electronic communication when I have more time to play.

John Dawes

Linking to the Internet – given a modern and fairly powerful computer – requires a modem to connect the computer to the telephone network and membership of an Internet service provider. The only costs thereafter are about £100 a year subscription plus an increased phone bill – but with ordinary care, this increase should be no more than a few pounds (less than ten) per month.

As well as enabling you to send e-mail to business contacts, the Internet offers access to thousands of pages of information on just about anything, and the opportunity to discuss common interests – to chat – with other Internet users. I do not, myself, have any need to despatch or receive material by e-mail and am not – but maybe that'll turn out to be a 'not yet' comment/attitude – convinced of the benefits, *to me*, of the information and discussion facilities available.

Investigate the Internet before signing up – you can try it out at 'cyber-cafes' and the like. For some writers it is probably worthwhile, but certainly not for all. Resist the blanket blandishments of sales staff and the over-enthusiastic advice of computer *nerds*.

Looking good – on paper

There are other aspects of looking good, looking business-like, than the ever-increasing growth in the use of electronic equipment. What first lands on an editor's or publisher's desk is usually a letter. A writer is a dealer in words, the letter is his or her ambassador or salesperson. A writer's letter must look good.

A business letter has to be 'headed'. The business-like writer needs to give careful thought to the design of his or her letterhead.

Letterheads

It used to be straightforward. If you wanted headed notepaper, you went to a specialist printer and they 'designed' a letterhead for you; it was usually one of half-a-dozen or so standard designs, all somewhat sedate. (Times, Italic or Handwriting fonts, block or staggered layout, etc.) The printer would usually urge you away from any too-outlandish design ideas – like incorporating artwork or unusual fonts. 'Too expensive, sir/madam.' (I even had difficulty in persuading one such printer to include a horizontal line beneath my heading.)

Today though, there are many people ready to design a letterhead for you, by playing around on their computer. Indeed, with most writers now owning their own computers, they can design their own letterhead, save it as a standard file and call it up every time they want to write a letter. There's no longer any need to keep a stock of headed notepaper.

This 'freedom' to design one's own letterhead is a mixed blessing. It may encourage the use of too many different fonts and the incorporation of inappropriate artwork from the too-readily available clip-art collections. Avoid these temptations. Your need to look professional means you must have a professional-looking letterhead.

A letterhead needs your name, your address (including 'England' or 'United Kingdom' if you sell work abroad) and your phone and fax number(s). If you indulge in e-mail, your electronic address should also be included. In my view, the letterhead does not need to say that you are a writer: this is either known or will quickly become clear. If you use a *known* pen-name, you may wish to include this, in smaller type, with your real name. Be sure that it is clear which is your real name and which the pen-name. (You want the cheques to be made out to the real you.)

I suggest that your name (first name, not initials) should be printed larger than the address, but not too large. Leave large names to shops and stores. On my own letterhead (*see* Figure 2.1), my name is in 12-point Arial Black and the address and tel/fax number is all in 8-point Univers bold.

Avoid using too many different fonts and sizes. Unless you do, the result will almost invariably turn out looking amateurish and unprofessional. I had intended to use 12-point Univers bold for my name, but it didn't look quite right – a bit 'skinny' – whereas Arial Black, which is a very similar bold *sans-serif* design but 'squatter', looked fine. My letters are all now typed in 11-point, 'non-bold', Univers. (Though I says it m'self, as shouldn't, my letters now look really good – even if the content ...) When laying out the letterhead, line up the heading with what will be the left margin of the future typescript.

Although, almost certainly your computer will offer you free relevant clip-art – of a quill pen, say, or someone sitting at a computer screen – it is wise to resist the temptation to incorporate such gimmicks in your letterhead. Let restraint be your watchword – at least in this area.

Just as I do not specify my profession (above), I do not subscribe to the inclusion of 'Member of the Society of Authors' or 'Member of the Romantic Novelists Association' or the like, in my letterhead. (I am in the first, but not the second.) Such letterhead-mentions will not enhance your sales, nor your *kudos*, so why bother? But there are other writers who would disagree with me. Your choice. If you decide that you do want to include such membership details, at least do it discreetly – use a small font.

That last point sums up my attitude to letterheads. They should be DISCREET. (And it's not that I would always advocate such discretion; in some aspects of the writing business I'm decidedly pushy and brash.)

Gordon Wells

Mon Repos   99 Chesterfield Road   Muddlecombe   East Muddlesex   TA72 9UD   England   Tel/Fax: 01999 123456

15 March 1999

Peter Day
Allison & Busby Ltd
114 New Cavendish Street
LONDON W1M 7FD

Dear Peter

As usual, at this time of the month, I enclose a Statem
both my 'author account' and my 'editorial adviser acc

That apart, you will wish to know that I met James Wi
Writers' Conference and talked about the possibility of
on Writing Romantic Fantasy, the up-and-coming new
of these and seems quite keen on the idea – but I'm no
understands what is involved in writing a How-to book
and try and extract a draft synopsis.

I also met Janie Humperdink who assured me that she'
manuscript of her book. She'll be delivering on time, no

That's all for now. Regards to Vanessa and Su. I'll be
and will call in – checking first.

Cheers

Gordon

Gordon Wells

Mon Repos   99 Chesterfield Road   Muddlecombe   East Muddlesex   TA72 9UD   England   Tel/Fax: 01999 123456

STATEMENT OF ACCOUNT

15 July 1999

The Writers' Quarterly
63 Wiltshire Road
Muddleton-on-Fees
East Muddlesex TA1 99PQ

Payment received during June, with thanks:

NIL

Payments outstanding:

Title	Submitted date	Published date	Payment due
Published, not yet paid for:			
Gordon's Page 1-99	201198	Jan 99	£00
Gordon's Page 2-99	050299	Apr 99	£00
Total outstanding			£00 - DUE
Delivered and accepted, not yet published:			
Gordon's Page 3-99	150599	(Jul 99	£00)
Awaiting despatch – on receipt of payment due:			
Gordon's Page 4-99		(Oct 99	£00)

Gordon Wells

Mon Repos   99 Chesterfield Road   Muddlecombe   East Muddl

INVOICE

15 March 1999

The Writers' Club Ltd
PO Box 269
Reigate Surrey RH1 6GP

INVOICE

To:

1800-word article WRITING A NON-FICTION BOOK,
accepted for future publication in *Foreword*.
(Oral acceptance at meeting, Jarman/Wells 9 March 1999.)   £00.00

No VAT registration.

Figure 2.1 My own letterhead (with mock address) as used for a typical business letter, an invoice and a statement of account – to illustrate layout and possible content.

Invoices and statements

Another of your stationery needs will inevitably be an invoice form. (Some magazines, some publishers, require invoices for every payment.) Beginning writers are often worried – unnecessarily – about how to prepare an invoice.

An invoice is no more than a bill for work done. Think of it as a simplified letter, stating what you have done and delivered and how much you expect to be paid for it. I use my standard letterhead for invoices (and for statements of account too). Figure 2.1 shows one of my business letters, a short invoice (illustrating the wording I use) and a typical statement of account.

A statement of account is a useful document when you are working regularly for one editor or publisher – and payments are due for more than one piece of work. For many years, I wrote a regular column in a magazine; payments tended to be rather slow in coming and a statement of account allowed me to remind the editor of which pieces had been paid for and which payments were still due (or overdue). A formal statement of account should show both payments made and payments due – most times I use my statements merely to remind of payments outstanding. But I also keep careful records of what is paid and when (*see* Chapter 6).

Business cards

Another item of stationery which some writers consider important is a business card. Without doubt, it is useful to have something readily available to hand to someone who wants a reminder of your name and address. Business cards are particularly useful/important if travelling overseas – in both America and the Far East they are near essential – one exchanges them as a form of ritual.

In Britain, if you are going to be visiting people unannounced or on first contact – seeking research information or an interview, for example – a card can undoubtedly be useful. In my own more mundane writing activities however, I have seldom felt the need for a card. (If anyone wants an immediate note of my address, I usually have a sticky label in my wallet with my name and address on it. Otherwise – (*see* Chapter 3) I believe in following up personal contacts with a confirming letter – which can go 'on file'. A letter is less likely to be mislaid than a wee piece of card.)

I have a business card which I change now and again – but it's more for flash than use

Jill Dick

Jill Dick B.A.

Member of the Society of Authors
NUJ member

Author & Journalist

phone: 01298 812305

e-mail: jillie@cix.compulink.co.uk

Oldacre
Horderns Park Road
Chapel-en-le-Frith
High Peak
SK23 9SY

A business card can be useful, and is more than an affectation. It also shows a business-like attitude when someone asks for your address or phone number. I once had one of mine done with my photo on it, which ensured that people remembered who I was, even if they forgot my name. This was not my original idea, but one copied from writers at the American conferences I have attended, where self-promotion is regarded as less of an ego trip that it is in Britain.

Jean Saunders

My business card is an Able-Label centred on a square of glossy coloured card. You might get a pink, blue or turquoise one, depending on my mood. I have never got around to something more professional. And no one's complained.

Stella Whitelaw

Still, personal choice aside, many writers like to carry cards. Once again, my own view is that a card should be discreet in its appearance – but there is much to be said for incorporating a tiny memory-jogging photograph of yourself in the card.

Writers working in the comics/picture-script field will sometimes indicate their speciality on their card – by a line drawing perhaps or an unattached speech-balloon 'saying' what they do. Again, I believe there is merit in this particular non-discreet approach.

Stationery

Stationery is, of course, of considerable importance to every writer. And not just in the form of headed note-paper (plus envelopes, of course) and business cards: a writer's actual work output is still basically words on paper.

It pays therefore to shop around for the best deals in stationery and other such purchasing. Buy paper in bulk – you will get a far better price if you buy ten reams at a time. (And don't forget, if you are using your computer to store your letterhead, you need blank paper for that.) I standardise – for all uses, letters, typescript, etc. – on good quality 80 gsm 'copier' paper. Business envelopes – primarily DL size (110 x 220 mm) – too are best bought in bulk, a thousand at a time. Yes, it sounds a lot initially, but they keep – and soon go.

I buy lever arch files (for correspondence) and flat card files (for complete book typescripts) in bulk too. Again, the consequent cost savings make it well worthwhile.

There are several discount stationery suppliers. I have always found Viking Direct – phone free on 0800-424444 for a catalogue – efficient, quick and usually the cheapest (especially if you pick the right sale catalogue from which to order). They also supply computer disks, printer refills, etc. Once you're on the Viking mailing list, you can expect a never-ending supply of monthly sale and other special catalogues.

ProFile 8

Writer Louise Cahill

Biog Louise is a journalist and photographer whose material has appeared in a variety of publications including the *Mail on Sunday* (*Night and Day*), *Manchester Evening News*, *Yorkshire Post*, *Bella*, *Scuba World*, *Nursery World* and *The Big Issue in the North*. She specialises in writing human interest, marine and travel features – and she loves interviewing. A member of the NUJ and the SWWJ, Louise won the *Writers News* 1995 Freelance Journalist of the Year award.

Credits include 'Captivated by Kerry' (*Cork Examiner* – her first paid feature), 'New kids on the kibbutz' (*Manchester Evening News*) and 'Taking the hump in Eilat' (*Yorkshire Post*).

Question Do you have a business card (as a writer) and is it useful?

My business card's extremely useful. On the front is a photograph (an under-water scene of fishes and coral, etc.) which I took in Eilat. This is one of my favourite photographs and appeared in a *Scuba World* feature – and on the Internet. I enjoy writing marine-based features, so my card's almost like my logo.

Because my card's unusual, it promotes a response, and is less likely to be discarded.

Louise Cahill

Member of the NUJ and the
Society of Women Writers and Journalists

10 Danesbury Rise Cheadle Cheshire SK8 1JW

Tel/Fax 0161 428 2884
Mobile 0589 499 618

Photograph Copyright Louise Cahill

Address labels

And finally, for 'keeping up appearances' on paper, every writer needs sticky name and address labels. In my view, the best supplier is undoubtedly the Able-Label firm, Steepleprint Ltd., Mallard Close, Earls Barton, Northampton NN6 0LS (Tel: 01604 810781). They've been in business now for many years; they're very reliable and, as far as I know, they're the cheapest. Don't forget that, as well as the little 19 x 40 mm 'back-of-the-envelope-or-cheque' labels, they can also supply 32 x 64 mm labels which are ideal for the ever-essential stamped addressed envelopes.

I've even seen the labels stuck on small cards – as DIY business cards.

3

SELLING YOURSELF

The successful and business-like writer is one with a steady flow of work. And one way of helping yourself along the road towards achieving that happy state is to 'be known'. If you hide your light under the proverbial bushel, it's unlikely to shine out.

If an editor or publisher is approached with an offer of work – article, short story or book – from a total unknown, the submission takes its chances in the 'slush pile' (the daily delivery of unsolicited material, much of which is inevitably unsuitable). But if the name of the submitting writer is even just vaguely familiar to the editor/publisher it stands a better chance of being looked at first. It may not stand a better chance of acceptance, but at least you get a speedy response. And waiting can be agony.

The (competent) writer with a high profile usually achieves more than the reticent mouse.

Of course, to have or adopt a high profile, you have to do something to have a high profile about. The business-like writer is the one who makes the most of every success, right from the start.

Scrapbook and/or portfolio

Your first article or short story has been accepted. Of course you will push it under the noses of all reachable family, friends and colleagues. That's only natural pride. But don't stop there. Make several photocopies of the published work – irrespective of the publication it's in (even an in-company newsletter or small press magazine). Magazine editors increasingly ask to see evidence of published work before giving a go-ahead for an article idea or looking at a short story. Right from the start, build up your 'portfolio'. (And in this respect, the writing world is doing no more than move closer to practice in the world of artists and photographers.)

> Value your work. Once you've a small portfolio, and are on your way to becoming established, realise if your work is good enough for publication, it must be paid for. Don't undersell yourself. Have confidence in, and be proud of your work.
>
> Louise Cahill

Keep at least one pristine copy of the actual published material too. Right from your very first appearance in print, you should keep a scrapbook. The first 'original' should go in the scrapbook; if you get hold of more copies keep them – perhaps in clear plastic pockets – against the need to make further photocopies as editorial 'credentials'. The alternative, of course, is for your scrapbook to be a folder of clear plastic pockets. Although this is an excellent way of displaying it, as a 'portfolio' – if you are ever lucky enough to get a face-to-face meeting with an editor – there can then be a danger of your losing/giving away that one precious original. If you lose your original it can sometimes be exceedingly difficult to replace.

In time, as your scrapbook builds up, you will leaf back through it and maybe note how your work has improved over the years. (On occasions, I wonder how some of my – very – early work got accepted, it's so awful.) A scrapbook is also a boon when you are depressed by a run of rejections: look back at your past acceptances. You did it then, you can do it again.

Another benefit of a scrapbook is its use as a research or reference source. You know that the facts in that article are correct: you researched them then, you don't need to re-research. You can write up a set of already-used facts differently and sell them in another article. Chapter 7 gives more information on serial rights – FBSR – and Chapter 8 on recycling your research.)

Personal press releases

As and when you sell your first book, make the most of it. Your publisher will mention it in his catalogue; he may run a small publicity campaign to launch it; if it's of any unusual interest, you might get a brief radio interview (on local radio); but often, it will attract little interest. A business-like writer will attempt to build up more interest – but check with your publisher before doing anything in the publicity line, to avoid any clashes.

Subject to the publisher-check, you might prepare and issue a press release to your local media – newspapers and radio stations. This can be along the lines of 'Local resident publishes first book at age of 77', or '... book on [subject]'. Write it in the third person, as though about someone else.

You need to find something interesting to say about yourself or the book – something just a wee bit *different* – and then MAKE THE MOST OF IT. Mention any 'names' that are in any way connected, and include a 'quote' from them if at all possible; emphasise also any local tie-in.

Head the press release ... PRESS RELEASE, and type it with big (maybe even extra-big) margins, and double spaced, just as you would any other typescript for publication.

Write all press releases 'top down' – i.e. make the most important point first. An editor may have a small space into which only part of your release will fit: he/she will simply cut your piece to size by deleting from the bottom up, short paragraph by short paragraph. (No paragraph should exceed 50 words.)

Overall, keep it short – about 200 words – and at the bottom, always include a prominent contact telephone number, as well as your name (with first name, *not* initials – the media's a first-names world) and address. Ideally, send a copy of the book's cover with the press release. If your book has particular relevance to another part of the country, send press releases to the media there too – but with a local slant.

Send out the press release before the book is published – but not too early (48 hours is usually about right) – mark it EMBARGOED UNTIL [publication date]. The media is accustomed to such advance news items and will (nearly always) respect the embargo.

If you tell the media later, it won't be news, it'll be history. If you tell them too early, there's a danger of your 'news' being filed and forgotten.

Send it out, well-timed, and await results. You may be lucky and be contacted for more information – or it may just die a death. Don't give up though. Your next press release may fare better.

Another opportunity for issuing a press release is if you are 'lucky' (it's never just luck – it takes ability) enough to win a prize for something you've written. Whether it's *only* a small short story or poetry competition – or being short listed for the Booker – you should make the most of it. Tell your local – or national, if it's really important – media about it, in a press release. (Once again though, check with the organisers of the competition that they are not already publicising your success.)

Personal PR brochures

Having discussed in the previous chapter the uses of business cards, there is another side of a writer's high profile that is worth considering now. As you write more, you may be asked to give talks about your work, your books, and their subjects; as far as possible, never turn down such requests. Indeed, it is worth seeking out opportunities to talk. Each time you give a talk you are increasing the number of people who are aware of your activities – and who, next time, will at least glance at a book with your name on the cover. Not only can you perhaps increase future sales, you can often sell your books on the spot at a speaking engagement. Don't be scared of such public speaking: Chapter 8 includes advice on how to go about it.

Whether responding to those wanting you to speak or seeking out more opportunities for yourself, a simple PR brochure about yourself and your books can be useful. Restrict such brochures to the two sides of an A4 sheet of paper. Design the sheet for folding twice – as with a business letter – so that the resultant brochure will fit neatly into a standard DL (110 x 220 mm) envelope. DL envelopes, accepting two-fold brochures, are markedly cheaper than C5 (130 x 65 mm) envelopes holding single-fold brochures.

ProFile 9

Writer Pamela Oldfield

Biog A full-time writer, Pamela Oldfield writes historical fiction for adults and books for children of all ages. She has published more than 70 books. When not actually writing, Pamela travels to research her books and also gives talks and workshops both in the UK and abroad. She has worked closely with the Kent Literary Festival and helped to set up the Short Story Competition run by the Metropole Arts Centre in Folkestone. More than half a million people borrow her books from libraries each year. She is now published by Piatkus Books.

Credits include for adults, *The Heron Saga* (four books about tin mining) and the hop picking trilogy; for children, *The Gumby Gang* series and the *Melanie Brown* books are firm favourites.

Question Do you have a personal PR brochure – and if so, for what purpose?

I produced my first publicity brochure with the help of a friend in graphics, and a professional printer. It cost then about £600 for 6,000 copies – cheaper per copy in large numbers. My mistake was to leave no space for up-dating the information. Consequently, after a few years, I abandoned the surplus and produced another, similar, but in a different colour, so that I could mention recently published novels. I use it as a handout at talks and workshops, when submitting material to editors, accompanying business letters where relevant, and when offering articles to magazines. (I almost never send out a writing CV, as the brochure is fairly comprehensive.)

The next brochure will be produced on my computer. That will mean they can easily be updated when a new book appears, and can be run off as needed – say fifty copies if I'm giving a talk. Because it will have to be black print, I shall use pastel coloured paper as a background; we'll fold them by hand. I think a good photograph helps, if you can manage it. It adds the personal touch.

ProFile 10

Writer Jill Paton Walsh

Biog After a brief spell as a school teacher, Jill Paton Walsh retired to start a family – and to write fiction for children. As a children's author, she has won many awards, including the Whitbread Prize, 1974, for *The Emperor's Winding Sheet* and the Smarties Grand Prix, 1984, for *Gaffer Samson's Luck*. She now also writes for adults. In 1994 her self-published adult novel, *Knowledge of Angels*, reached the shortlist for the Booker Prize.

In 1996 Jill Paton Walsh received the CBE for services to literature.

Credits include *Knowledge of Angels*, (US publisher, Houghton Mifflin), *The Serpentine Cave*, *A School for Lovers* and two crime novels including *The Wyndham Case*. Also, the 1984 Universe Prize for her children's book, *A Parcel of Patterns*.

Question Do you have a personal PR brochure – and if so, for what purpose?

I have two PR brochures – a now out-of-date glossy one for children's books, and a current one for adult work. The current one, which can be printed off as required at home, and kept up-to-date is much more practical than the glossy colour-printed one. Both are my own work, and were paid for by me.

I use the brochures to distribute free to audiences to whom I speak (it helps them find one's books later) and to deal with the endless flow of letters requesting information, or commenting on books. I strongly recommend this simple personal promotion to fellow authors. If you get a brochure professionally designed and printed the cost is allowable against tax; if you make them yourself they are inexpensive and flexible. The only caveat I would make is to be sure they look reasonably good; an untidy one or an ugly one would do one a disservice,

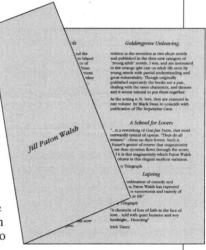

Unless you are artistically inclined it might be wise to seek the assistance of someone who is, in the design of your brochure. And be clear about the purpose of the brochure: if it's to hand out to all and sundry, you may not want your address and phone number on it; if for issue only to potential hirers, then their inclusion is obviously wise. If the brochure is to publicise your services – from after-dinner talks to day-long courses or literary criticism – remember that your fees will need regular updating. Because of the expense of printing the main brochure, it's a good idea to put the prices on a separate one-third-A4 insert sheet.

Include reproductions of the covers of some of your books in the brochure; most people will decide to include a photograph of themselves too. Favourable reviewers' comments are also worth including. And always, a brief – say 200 words at most – third-person biography of you as a writer. (When 'selling yourself' as a writer, it is seldom necessary to refer to other facets of your life.)

A writer's CV

When first approaching publishers – and sometimes, magazine editors – it can be useful to include a curriculum vitae, a CV. A PR brochure as above is ideal for distribution to those outside the writing/publishing world. But it is a *publicity* document. A writer's CV serves a different purpose. It is less flamboyant, more factual, and can perhaps be varied in accordance with the target recipient. (Sometimes it need be little more than a few paragraphs within an introductory letter to a publisher.)

Begin your CV, like any other, with your name, address, phone/fax numbers and – depending on the addressee – your date of birth and list of academic qualifications (from GCSEs to PhDs – and in that order). Again, depending on who you are sending the CV to, and the relevance of the information to the recipient, a short summary list of your writing experience.

The comment on writing experience need not be particularly detailed – unless there is very little of it, and you need to make it look more. It could be something like, 'I have had a number of

I keep an up-to-date CV but find it more useful for dealing with the Press than with publishers. There is nothing more embarrassing that being half-way through an interview and forgetting the title of your latest book. Believe me, I've done it. The point is, the newly published one that they want to talk about is not the one I'm currently working on, and may not be the one I was working on before that. Of course, having an agent I don't have to approach publishers cold – if I did it would make sense to have something cogent to open a pitch with.

Jo Bannister

I prefer sales leaflets to CVs. I keep *me* in the background in favour of my books first. As I am primarily an author-publisher, I do all my own work in print and vary the blurb to suit the publication.

John Dawes

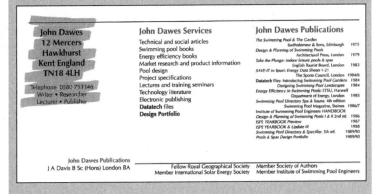

John Dawes
12 Mercers
Hawkhurst
Kent England
TN18 4LH

Telephone 0580 753146
Writer • Researcher
Lecturer • Publisher

John Dawes Services
Technical and social articles
Swimming pool books
Energy efficiency books
Market research and product information
Pool design
Project specifications
Lectures and training seminars
Technology literature
Electronic publishing
Datatech files
Design Portfolio

John Dawes Publications
The Swimming Pool & The Garden
  Bartholomew & Sons, Edinburgh 1975
Design & Planning of Swimming Pools
  Architectural Press, London 1979
Take the Plunge: indoor leisure pools & spas
  English Tourist Board, London 1983
SAVE-IT in Sport: Energy Data Sheets 1-21
  The Sports Council, London 1984/6
Datatech files: Introducing Swimming Pool Gardens 1984
  Designing Swimming Pool Landscapes 1984
Energy Efficiency in Swimming Pools: ETSU, Harwell
  Department of Energy, London 1985
Swimming Pool Directory Spa & Sauna. 4th edition
  Swimming Pool Magazine, Staines 1986/7
Institute of Swimming Pool Engineers HANDBOOK
Design & Planning of Swimming Pools I & II 2nd ed. 1986
ISPE YEARBOOK Preview 1987
ISPE YEARBOOK & Update III 1988
Swimming Pool Directory & Specifier. 5th ed. 1989/90
Pools & Spas Design Portfolio 1989/90

John Dawes Publications
J A Davis B Sc (Hons) London BA

Fellow Royal Geographical Society
Member International Solar Energy Society

Member Society of Authors
Member Institute of Swimming Pool Engineers

I always enclose a CV to a new-to-me publisher. It's usually a photocopy of one of my How-to book covers, which have a very nice personal piece – and means I haven't made it up. A shortened form is often, quite simply ... CV: 30 published books, 211 published short stories. And that's all I put.

Stella Whitelaw

feature articles on [associated book subject] published in such magazines as *Cosmopolitan*, *The Lady* and *Dog Monthly*.' Alternatively, 'I am already a well-published author with some 30 erotic novels to my credit, published by Muddleford University Press.' Or, 'I have had a few articles published in my firm's in-house magazine.' Note the brief writing biogs in the ProFiles throughout this book: model yours on these.

The CV must be immaculately presented: it should be clearly laid out – ideally on a single sheet – and quick and easy to read.

Attached to, but separate from your CV, you should, if appropriate, provide a list of published book titles. Be consistent: list them in date order or reverse date order; list fiction and non-fiction titles separately; include publisher's name and the year of first publication. If there are several editions, give date – and publisher, if different – of each.

Meeting people

No matter how impressive your CV or PR brochure, there is no substitute for making contacts in person – face to face. Fine, but how and where?

In America there are many regular conferences and conventions when readers (fans), writers, editors, agents and publishers get together and 'network'. In Britain we are less lucky: we don't have such broad-interest conventions. We have to make do with writers' conferences, at which we can sometimes meet up with guest editors and/or publishers, and book fairs, notably the London International Book Fair, each spring. The LIBF is primarily intended for publishers' sales teams to display their wares to booksellers and librarians, but writers can attend, albeit somewhat on sufferance.

But maybe I am a little unfair on our British conferences and the London Book Fair. They may attract a less comprehensive range of professionals than their American counterparts – but they probably have a more friendly overall atmosphere.

Most UK writers' conferences are weekend events with less than 100 people in attendance: there will often be two or three editors, publishers or agents among those attending. (The two biggest

British writers' annual conferences – the marvellous Writers' Summer School for 300-plus writers at Swanwick and the Writers' Holiday at Caerleon, both in mid-summer – are each near-week-long, with proportionately more opportunities for making useful contacts. For a place at Swanwick, contact Brenda Courtie on 01327 262477; for Caerleon, Anne Hobbs on 01633 854976.) And it is usually possible for writers to approach the editors, agents, etc., introduce themselves and chat – briefly.

> Writers' conferences are marvellous for making new contacts, sometimes through speakers, and sometimes through writing friends and acquaintances. My first non-fiction book (Allison & Busby, this series) was a direct result of talking with Gordon Wells at a conference. I have also many times been approached at conferences to speak at writers' circles or other events, either because I am speaking at the current one, or have been recommended by other people.
>
> Jean Saunders
>
> I've never had a commission through attending a conference, but I have several times sold things to people met – editors of anthologies, foreign publishers – who might otherwise not have bought from me.
>
> Susan Moody

All you can hope to do in such circumstances is to make yourself known, mention your interests or specialisms and arrange to send something later, by post. It is debatable whether it is sensible or worthwhile on such occasions, to hand over a copy of your PR brochure, or of your CV. In my view, editors and publishers are only human (yes, really): they're just as likely as you or I to mislay anything they're given in a social setting. Personally, I don't even hand over a business card – I just get a letter of confirmation off as soon as possible. If there is not too long an interval between introduction and delivery of samples, you will have achieved enough – the editor, or whoever will vaguely remember the person associated with the name on the submission.

And remember: if you hog the time of an editor, publisher or agent for too long, you are in danger of:

- boring them – and thus making yourself a less attractive prospect, and
- preventing others from having their chance to speak to them. (Do unto others ...).

But there are many other worthwhile opportunities for 'networking' at the British conferences: writer to writer. On the whole, writers are a friendly and helpful bunch: most will willingly share market and other information – who is looking for what, etc. – and maybe, ideas; most will offer generous and unstinting advice to beginning writers – just don't ask them to take time out to read and criticise your work.

The London International Book Fair is a different occasion. The exhibition halls at London's Olympia are filled by publishers' stands, displaying forthcoming titles. It is a sales show. Only occasionally, and briefly, do the editorial side of a publisher's team show up. But although writers are there, more or less on sufferance, it is a good opportunity to see what's going on in the publishing world. You can pick up publishers' catalogues by the dozen – and all in one day. (More than one day and you'll be dead on your feet.) And maybe you can get ideas for future books and approaches.

As a direct result of speaking to someone on the Henderson Publishing stand a few years ago, I offered them a book idea. That first idea was turned down but – maybe because my submission/approach was professional – a little later, I was asked to write a different book for them. I've done several more for them since then. I'm glad I worked my footsore way around the Book Fair that year.

Whoever you meet – editor, publisher or agent – and wherever, it's essential to FOLLOW UP on the meeting. Don't give them time to forget you. If they agreed to look at your work, get it to them within days. And remind them of the meeting. Leave it all for a month while you pluck up courage and ... you're dead, forgotten.

Agents

Having mentioned agents, consider their role and their advantages.

A literary agent is just 'what it says on the tin'. They act as a go-between in literary matters, looking after their clients' interests. A good agent can be the best thing that ever happens to a writer: they can ensure that the writer gets the best financial deal possible; they can offer the writer a shoulder to cry on when work is going badly; they can protect the thin-skinned writer from the brash world of commerce. A bad – or incompatible – agent can on the other hand inhibit and/or drag a writer down. A bad agent might negotiate poor deals and perhaps block off further sales opportunities.

Increasingly, some publishers are declining first-book offers other than those submitted by agents. This is because those

> My agent is such a part of my life that if she decided to try another line of work I would be utterly bereft. She is one of that rare breed of agents who is a tiger when it comes to making sales and an artist when it comes to creative input.
>
> Susan Moody

> The only sure way to get an agent is to write something marketable!
>
> Pamela Oldfield

> As a specialist writer I doubt if any agent would take me on – anyway, I much prefer direct contacts.
>
> John Dawes

> I don't and never have had an agent. Harlequin Mills and Boon have their own very successful foreign sales set-up. I can see an agent might be useful when discussing the vexed question of money with publishers, as authors are notoriously bad at this. If I ever wrote a different kind of book for another market, I would probably offer it to an agent – if I could find one, which is by no means certain in these uncertain times.
>
> Anne Ashurst

ProFile 11

Literary agent (and author) Dorothy Lumley

Biog Dorothy Lumley's first job was as editorial assistant on a reference magazine. She was then paperback editor at New English Library and, after a year as a freelance editor, worked her way to editorial director at Methuen/Magnum Paperbacks. She then worked for Laurence Pollinger Literary Agency before moving to Devon and launching her own Dorian Literary Agency in 1986. She is also a published writer of romantic fiction.

Question What are you looking for when considering whether or not to take on a new writer – and what do you look for when considering a book?

Taking on a new writer, I look to the long term. I don't want a one-off writer. It takes time to find out if the relationship will work, if you can 'get on' and the relationship will become productive work-wise.

However, the final arbiter is always: have I enjoyed what I read and do I see it as marketable. I will err on the side of marketable. I can enjoy something because it is successful at what it sets out to achieve, even if personally I wouldn't buy it for private reading. So the first three chapters of a novel must be readable, and introduce the main character(s) – with whom I can get involved, and care about enough to continue reading. (It must always be the first two or three chapters – if you don't think they are your best, then rewrite them until they are as good as the rest of your novel.) That said, I may reject things that are well written if I have lots of authors already working in that area, e.g. fantasy, whereas I'll pay attention to something I don't have, or don't have enough of, e.g. westerns, mainstream.

Non-fiction: a very detailed proposal, with full chapter breakdown, is essential, plus one chapter (I suppose not necessarily the first, though it helps) plus a paragraph on how this particular book will either fill an empty niche, or be controversial or up-to-date enough to replace existing books. Also, I'm afraid, it 'Helps to Be Famous' – which is the title of my contribution on non-fiction publishing to *Instead of Full Stops* (Ed. Susan Sellers, Women's Press). In order to generate media attention, publishers prefer non-fiction writers to have built up a reputation of some kind in their chosen field.

I offer quite a lot of editing, as that is my background and I enjoy it. But I don't force it on a client.

publishers, inundated with mostly unpublishable material, are relying on agents to reject the dross and only offer them worthwhile and relevant manuscripts. It costs publishers a lot even just to skim through the 'slush pile' – the unsolicited manuscripts – and send most of them back.

There is therefore an added incentive for a wannabe writer to be 'agented'. But it can be as hard to find a good agent willing to take you on as to find a publisher.

There was no need to have an agent for short story writing, which I did for some ten years before writing my first novel. By then I still didn't see the need for an agent. This changed, but not before I had published 17 novels on my own, and because I felt I knew the publishing work quite well, and was perfectly able to discuss matter with editors, etc., I was still resistant to the idea. But then an American publisher I approached preferred to negotiate through an agent instead of directly with an author. At the time, this was pretty galling, as I had already made the initial approaches and virtually sold the novel myself.

But if I wanted that book to be published in America, I had to give in, and the agent and I worked amicably enough for some years, until we clashed on a non-fiction book that I wanted to write. It was the end of our association, and from then on, I've worked alone.

Contrary to popular belief, relatively few publishers insist on your having an agent. I do think it's also a very personal choice. Some writers prefer the close contact with publishers, while others need the buffer of a go-between, and would be hesitant to ask for a change of contract terms.

For new writers, a query letter to a suitable agent found in The Writers' Handbook or The Writers' & Artists' Yearbook, with a brief description of your work and aims is a good way to approach an agent of your choice. Asking other writers about their agents is also a good way of knowing if he or she is going to suit you, because it's very much a two-way relationship. Any author needs to find an agent who is totally compatible with what they want to do, and this isn't always the case. On the plus side, agents are in business to earn their percentages, so they will also get the best possible deals for you.

Jean Saunders

How do you tell a good agent from a bad one? The best way is to discuss agents with other writers. Find out which agents are popular – and ideally, get an introduction from a contented author to his or her agent. The next best way of finding a good agent is to meet and talk to them at conferences, etc., and decide you like the sound of them. The next way of finding an agent is to consult the standard writers' reference books and approach one who is a full member of the Association of Authors' Agents. (Membership at least guarantees a professional approach to agenting: it does not guarantee personal compatibility. Dip your toe in slowly.)

Before approaching an agent it is worth recognising how they make their living. Agents take a percentage – usually 10 per cent but edging up to 15 – from the earnings of each of their clients. For that percentage, agents negotiate with publishers on behalf of their authors. If you have written an obviously one-off book of only marginal importance, unlikely to attract more than a small advance (a few hundred pounds, say) and with insignificant royalties probably spread over a period of years, the agent's percentage is unlikely to cover their costs. Agents will be slow to sign up such an author. Similarly with a first novel, unlikely to become a bestseller, from someone who looks like a one-book author.

I both have an agent, and send work out on my own. Many agents don't handle short stories any more. I send these out myself. Magazine editors know my name and in most cases the stories are read fairly promptly. I need an agent for some genres which will not be looked at by a publisher unless submitted through an agent. It's not necessary to have an agent for Mills & Boon; an agent cannot get you any more money if your book is accepted by them. During a 'between agents' period, I sold several books on my own, so it's not impossible.

The only way to get an agent is to send them samples of your best work, meet them at conferences and talks, try to make a personal contact. Don't bore them with long, sad tales of writing woe. Be fresh, direct, to the point – and keep your word.

Stella Whitelaw

ProFile 12

Writer Jo Bannister

Biog Jo Bannister left school at 16 – with nine O-levels and the RSA Bronze Medal for English. She began working for a local newspaper in Northern Ireland and was joint runner-up as Young Journalist of the Year (British Press Awards) in 1976. After a spell as deputy editor of a local newspaper, she became editor in 1984 but left in 1987 to pursue her career as a writer. As well as a number of short stories, she has 17 published novels, including several in the Allison & Busby Crime series.

Credits include *A Bleeding of Innocents*, *Sins of the Heart* (Macmillan/Allison & Busby), and more recently, *The Primrose Convention* and *Broken Lines* (Macmillan).

Question Do you have an agent? Is he/she useful/helpful?

A good agent is the best tool a writer has or can acquire. Writing books and selling them are two different jobs and not many people are particularly good at two jobs. My agent gives me invaluable editorial advice without trying to alter what or how I write; supports me in any disagreements with my publishers (which have been happily rare); seeks out new markets for my work both at home and abroad; and negotiates sound practical contracts. In short, she does all the things I would have most trouble doing for myself. I can honestly say I don't begrudge her her cut. I'm certain I'd end up with a lower income by keeping 100 per cent of what I could negotiate for myself.

Agents want clients who will *continue* to produce saleable – and increasingly-saleable – work; it becomes progressively easier to sell the work of known authors.

Bearing the above in mind, when approaching an agent in the hope of their taking you on, you should give some indication of your future potential. Show enthusiasm. Not many shy little mice reach the best-seller lists. You need to sell yourself to an agent. Make them want to take YOU on. And that's as well as demonstrating your writing ability.

Pen-names

Having begun this chapter by recommending that authors adopt a 'high profile', let's end it at the other extreme: the use of a pseudonym – a pen-name.

As, for many years, a writer solely of non-fiction, I seldom saw the need for adopting a pen-name. I was writing about subjects I knew and had some expertise in; there were obvious advantages in consistently using my own name. My name became 'known' – and there was a limited but welcome spin-off from my writing activities to my 'day job'. It became known that I wrote about certain aspects of my work – and my work-place.

I use a pen-name because it keeps me separate from him. I can sell him easier than me, and I know how I have to react when I hear my pen-name used over the phone or see it on a display of my products. Essential to exist.

John Dawes

But, even then, there were occasions when it became necessary for me to adopt a pseudonym, or to choose to write without a by-line. Nearly always, in those days, it was because I was contributing too many features to a single issue of a magazine. (The same situation occasionally still arises nowadays.)

When I branched out, recently, into writing children's fiction, I saw no reason to adopt a pen-name. But some years ago, when I tried – unsuccessfully – to write a romance, and later a crime novel, I decided that discretion was the better part ... and adopted a pen-name. I judged that the writing field I was trying to break into was so very different from the one in which I was already, to some extent established, that a fresh – and anonymous – start was best. As it happened, I was not a success, and therefore it didn't matter.

Today, I wouldn't bother – but in any case, there are no by-lines for the picture-stories I've been writing for D C Thomson's COMMANDO books.

Those who write mainly fiction are the most likely to adopt pen-names. There are several excellent reasons for so doing.

ProFile 13

Writer Anne Ashurst (who writes as Sara Craven)

Biog Anne Ashurst was a professional journalist on various provincial newspapers before beginning her career as a novelist in 1975. Her first novel – *Garden of Dreams* – was accepted straight away. She now has over 50 contemporary romantic novels published by Harlequin Mills and Boon. (Her books are published in American in Harlequin Presents.) Divorced, with a grown-up son and daughter, she lives in Somerset with two small noisy terriers. In 1997, Anne won the last BBC TV *Mastermind* contest.

Credits include *Island of the Heart*, *Flawless*, *Storm Force* and *Deceived*. (All Harlequin Mills and Boon).

Question Why do you use a pen-name for your writing?

I used a pen-name from the moment I started for Harlequin Mills and Boon. At that time, I was a working journalist with a regular theatre column in my own name, and I wanted to keep the two things entirely separate.

I think, too, that a pen-name affords a certain amount of privacy for a novelist. Outside of the profession, very few people know who I am, or what I do, and I like it that way.

- Their early books are written for a low-paying, less prestigious publisher, whose contracts (*see* Chapter 7) include the right to first refusal of later books – and they wish to get out of this trap. (In defence of this clause in a publisher's contract, there is a risk in taking on a first-time author and the publisher may invest time and money to establish the author's name.)
- They may be writing so many (saleable) books that one publisher cannot handle the quantity. At the same time the publisher may not wish another publisher to gain 'spin-off' publicity advantage. So, the author writes for Publisher No. 2 under a different name. (Sometimes, it is the author's over-exposure that concerns the publisher: he/she may then write under a pen-name *for the same publisher*.) Such pen-names are often publicly disclosed later.
- They may be writing different types of novels, different genres, and not wish to confuse a loyal readership. A reader of cosy

romances might be horrified to pick up a new book by a favourite author – and find a raunchy bedroom romp or Elizabethan bodice-ripper. (Or maybe not.)

- They may wish to avoid confusion with a related day job – it might be inappropriate for a known fiction writer to be working as a news reporter.

And, to my mind, the least valid reason ...

- They may not wish family, friends and acquaintances to know that they are writing novels. (I'm proud of what I write. If you are not, it's time you made your work better – and worthy of pride.)

> I've used a pen-name, but not often. Mainly to help support ailing editors who don't want readers knowing who is behind the copy on so many pages. Make sure your correct name is on the cheque.
>
> Jill Dick

Irrespective of the reasons, it is certainly not unusual for an author's pen-names to be known within the profession. They are frequently shown on business cards and on letterheads. It is only the public who are sometimes kept in the dark. Few authors keep news of their successes from fellow authors.

It definitely pays to adopt a high profile – even with one or more pen-names.

4

IN TOUCH WITH BUYERS

Although personal contacts are ideal for introductions, they need written follow-ups. And although there are occasional opportunities for face to face meetings with magazine editors, first approaches by article or short story writers are most likely to be in writing. (Sometimes by phone, see below, but I don't recommend this for initial contacts.)

It used to be that article-writers selected their target magazine, wrote their thousand-word piece, and submitted it on spec. But, just as book publishers have found it too expensive to cope with the slush pile, so too, increasingly, have magazine editors. (Once again, because so much of the material magazine editors are offered is quite unsuitable.)

Instead of relying on agents (at least for their article needs) many magazine editors now follow the American practice of asking for query letters or article outlines rather than considering unsolicited complete pieces. On the whole, the Americans seem to prefer a hard-selling query letter; British practice favours a separate sheet, giving the outline of a proposed article.

Article outlines

An article outline should suggest the title and length of the proposed feature article and include the 'hook' – the opening paragraph or two – plus an idea of the aspects to be covered in the rest of the article and the way these will be treated – the 'slant'. It may also be necessary or helpful to give your 'credentials' for writing the article and the time you will need to complete and deliver it. Mention too, the availability of photographs or other illustrations.

Presentationally, the outline should be restricted to a single, well-laid-out sheet of A4 – and in this case, in single-spaced typescript. It is a good idea – certainly when preparing an outline for more technical/factual, rather than descriptive, articles – to present the content items as a list of bullet points. Put your name and address at the foot of the sheet – don't rely on this already being in the covering letter. The brief covering letter should then be restricted to a note of what is enclosed – and, surprisingly, many editors will consider more than one outline at a time. (Identify such editors – by experience with earlier single approaches – before trying multiple offers. In other words, only with editors who already know you and your work.) And of course, as always, enclose a stamped, self-addressed envelope for the editorial response.

Figure 4.1 shows one way of presenting a typical general interest feature outline.

Until an editor knows you and your work well, you will seldom get a commission on the basis of an outline. You are more likely to get a tentative go-ahead: 'That sounds interesting. I'd like to see the finished article.' Generally though, as long as you live up to the promise of the outline, such a go-ahead is close to an acceptance. Complete the offered article, get it in as soon as possible – and remind the editor of his/her earlier interest.

Many magazine editors also now ask for examples of similar, already published feature articles before giving a go-ahead on an outline. Refer back to the previous chapter for the need to build up such a 'portfolio'. But if you haven't yet had *similar* work accepted, send in a copy of anything you've had published; and if you've not yet reached even that stage ... just send in the outline anyway. The go-ahead may be slightly more tentative but if the idea's good, that's all. And once you've sold the first 'similar' article, you're up and running.

Once you become well-known to a magazine editor you can try querying ideas by phone. It is then even more important that you are thoroughly business-like in your approach. Editors are always busy. Prepare your query before you phone and explain your idea clearly and succinctly – if it's suitable you could well get a go-ahead. Waffle vaguely and you'll probably get a rejection.

Article outline

PROXY POCKETS

Gordon Wells

Today's Mr. Nippon, businessman, carries pens, slimline diary, etc., in the pockets of his immaculate suit. Young Joe Japan stuffs cash and credit cards into the pockets of his jeans – like youngsters everywhere.

It was not always so. In the eighteenth century Japanese men's clothes … had no pockets. To make matters worse, they didn't just sign papers: they made their 'mark' by stamping papers with a personally designed seal, which they carried around with them. They also carried around the ink for their seal.

Without pockets, they carried their few, small, everyday essentials – and the ink – in tiny boxes. Often highly decorative, these boxes, called <u>inro</u> – meaning 'seal container' – are extremely collectable today.

To follow:

- explanation of how <u>inro</u> carried, leading to descriptions of …
- <u>inro</u>, <u>ojme</u> and <u>netsuke</u> – with pronunciation
- various types of <u>netsuke</u>, the materials of which they are made, and some of the subjects portrayed
- difference – and how to differentiate (look for <u>himetoshe</u>) between practical statuette <u>netsuke</u> and shelf ornament <u>netsuke</u>.

To be illustrated with black and white photographs of <u>inro</u>, <u>ojme</u> and several <u>netsuke</u> (photographs by the writer). Sample photocopy of one photograph enclosed.

To make 1000-word article – plus choice from, say, four or five illustrations.

Note: I have my own, sizeable collection of netsuke, plus a number of <u>inro</u> and <u>ojme</u>. For many years, I have studied their history, design, etc.

Gordon Wells. 99 Chesterfield Rd, Muddlecombe, E Muddlesex TA72 9UD

---

*Figure 4.1: One – recommended – way of submitting an article outline or query. This would, of course, be accompanied by a **brief** covering letter – and a stamped addressed envelope.*

Writing to publishers

Whether or not you have already made face to face contact with a publisher, you need to write to them about your book, be it fiction or non-fiction.

Few publishers nowadays will look at more than a fairly detailed synopsis plus, initially, the first two or three chapters of a novel from a new author. There should also, of course, be a covering letter which can usefully include some personal information – full- or part-time writer, other published work, future aims, etc. (Refer back to the advice on CVs in Chapter 3.) Some publishers though, prefer to receive just an introductory letter, from which they then decide whether or not to call for the synopsis and sample chapters. In that situation, the introductory letter has to explain, briefly but EXCITINGLY, why the novel will interest them. Once again, you have to SELL yourself, and your work.

With non-fiction books – which should not usually be written before a publisher has expressed at least a firm interest – the best approach is initially to send selected publishers:

- a one- or two-page draft synopsis of the proposed book, and
- a one-page appraisal of the need and market for the book, a statement of who it is aimed at, and an explanation of the author's 'credentials' in respect of this particular book, plus
- a brief covering letter inviting them to call for (preferably author-specified) sample chapters and/or discussion of the synopsis.

(One reason why a non-fiction should be 'sold' before it is written is because a publisher will often wish to mould the book format/treatment to suit his list. Maybe the publisher has a series into which, with relatively small treatment modifications, the proposed book will fit. It is also possible that an interested publisher may wish to vary the overall coverage – and the non-fiction author will usually benefit from the publisher's fresh consideration of the project. If the book is already written, making the changes may be more difficult.)

ProFile 14

Publisher Peter Day, Allison & Busby

Biog After a wartime education, managed to become a lawyer the hard way in the 1950s, specialising in women's domestic rights. Then followed working for Amnesty in its early days, then Equity, and co-writing a book on Hispanic-American revolutionary movements in the 18th and 19th centuries, which led to publishing at Michael Joseph. He runs an international literary journal, in English, French and Spanish, *Pen International*, for International PEN, funded by UNESCO and Editorial Prensa Iberica. He has been the publisher of Allison & Busby, now in its 30th year, since the 1980s, either independently, or under the auspices of first W H Allen, then Virgin Publishing, and now Editorial Prensa Iberica – under which it is once again developing its full potential.

Question How do you like to be approached by an unagented new writer – and what do you look for when considering a book?

Today, publishers receive so many scripts that a number of them are refusing unsolicited works. Personally I have always found these rewarding but, given the pressure of time, and the cost of returning scripts, I have had to cut back. With fiction I now only accept a detailed synopsis, two sample chapters and a covering letter – which should also include a *brief* CV. The same applies for non-fiction works but, additionally, I would expect the non-fiction author to show why he/she is the person to write the book and its relevance in the marketplace. If, for example, it were a biography of Sir Walter Raleigh, how does it differ from previous biographies of Raleigh, is there room for another, and when was the last one published?

As the book being offered is by a new writer, it would not be 'author-led', so I would need to consider the completed work. No one these days, except in extraordinary circumstances (e.g. a very famous household name), commissions a fiction work from an unknown new writer. In non-fiction, it may be different if a new writer is producing a book on a subject which is highly topical, or he/she is uniquely placed to write it, or again, is a household name. In that case a non-fiction book may be commissioned on the basis of a synopsis and sample chapter. Otherwise the whole script would need to be considered.

Where one is in doubt when considering a full script, then the amount of editorial work involved and/or the 'attitude' of the author may be material. But usually these matters are not important if the script itself is gripping and saleable.

Letter-writing

Face to face introductions apart, a writer's letter is thus the first contact point with an editor or publisher. Think of your letter as your ambassador, your shop-window. A sloppy, unbusiness-like, imprecise letter gives the impression of a sloppy, unprofessional writer. After all – *words are our business.*

So ... how to write a better letter?

For a letter to be effective, it should be planned. To plan it, you need to consider:

- the reader: the person to whom you are writing – possibly not the formal addressee. What level of understanding can they be expected to have? (Editors and publishers know their job – don't 'teach grandma'.) Have you already met – remind the reader – or do you need to introduce yourself?
- your purpose in writing: of which more below. Too often, a writer is not really clear in his/her own mind just why they are writing the letter – the purpose determines the way the letter is written.
- what you are going to write: the content. Unless a letter is very short and simple, it may be worth listing the points to be made before starting – as you might, for instance, with a feature article. This, of course, links with ...
- the structure: the sequence in which you can best make the points in the content. It is often a good idea to end a letter with a (polite) request for the required action.

To write an effective letter you must be clear as to its purpose. What effect is the letter supposed to achieve? Be clear in your purpose – what you are trying to do – and your letter will always be better. Your purpose is probably one – or several, but linked – of the following:

- to *establish*, *maintain* or *improve* a business/professional relationship;
- to *create* a good impression of yourself in the reader's mind;
- to *inform* the reader – in order ...
- to *persuade* the reader to take some course of action – accept

your story or article, accept or commission your book or whatever work you are offering.

The first two are important initially; the latter two are usually the most important in an ongoing relationship. It often helps if the purpose can be stated – couched perhaps in less-than-bald terms – at the start of the letter.

The letter itself should be written in clear and simple terms: the 'usual' short words, short sentences and short paragraphs. Make very sure that there are no spelling or grammatical mistakes in your letter – and don't rely solely on your computer's spell-check, they can easily accept correctly spelt wrongly used words. Where practical, use bullet-points to list points to be made – as above.

Strive – HARD – to accommodate the whole letter on a single sheet of (headed – *see* Chapter 2) paper, and lay it out with plenty of white space around the text. Try to roughly centre the letter-proper – the text – on the page. As far as possible, allow wide margins. If you cannot avoid extending beyond a single page, make sure that the second page is identified. (My own practice is to show the addressee's name, my surname, the date and the page number, in a single underlined line, spread across the page, on second and – perish the thought – subsequent pages.)

Nowadays, the most commonly used layout for a business letter is 'fully blocked' – everything aligned to the left. (Refer back to Figure 2.1 page 36) That is, the date, references (if any), recipient's name and address, salutation, letter text, complimentary close and signatory's name (because most signatures are unintelligible) all start at the left margin with neither indent nor centring. More optional, there is a school of thought that advises against right justification on the grounds that unjustified text is easier to read. Depending on the amount of formality in the letter, it is sometimes sensible to include a title (after the salutation, before the text) to help focus the recipient's attention. Leave at least one and preferably two line-spaces between each of the main elements – addressee, salutation, text, etc. – in the letter. Leave one line-space between (un-indented) paragraphs.

> I write 'effective' letters which means bullets for significant items of information, attractive layout on the page, double spacing on occasions, to increase legibility. The notepaper itself is headed with a simple design and my name. It is vital to appear professional on paper. First impressions MATTER. Give yourself a fighting chance.
>
> Pamela Oldfield

Once again: in this writing business even more than elsewhere, your letter is your shop-window. Present yourself in an unbusiness-like fashion and the recipient of your letter is prejudiced against you from the start.

Filing

Still with letters – they are often (or should be treated as) important documents. A business-like writer stores those received, and copies of those sent, for future reference – and that means having files and a filing system.

For most writers this filing system – the mere thought of which makes some take fright – can be simple and straightforward. My own system is merely to put all writing and 'writing-personal' correspondence – in and out – in a lever arch file in date order. (I keep another lever arch file for correspondence about my lecturing/talking activities.) I file only correspondence in this file – and each file lasts me about three months before it is full, which means I have a shelf-full of full files. I have other files for copies of articles, and a whole series of cheaper flat files, one for each book. The big advantage of my 'system' is that it is simple. I would possibly be better served if I were to open separate date-order files for each addressee – I don't have that many – but I'm lazy.

I do though, mark the 'date received' on each incoming letter and cross reference it to my letter to which it relates. On my 'original' letter, I also note the reply date. With these annotations, I can find my way back through the files.

On the subject of filing, it is also wise to establish a system to organise the files held on the computer's disk(s). I seldom retain computer-file copies of letters, other than really important ones – and these usually only until their subject matter has been sorted out – but there are many other files to organise.

Writing, as I do, articles, picture-scripts, fiction and non-fiction books – plus reader's reports for Allison & Busby – I have separate directories (in 'old-fashioned MS-DOS-speak') or folders (in 'Windows 95-speak') for articles, picture-scripts, and books. Within the respective directories/folders there are sub-folders for each individual book – and sometimes for 'bulky' groups of associated articles, such as a regular column. Although Word 97 allows longer-than-eight-character file titles, I still keep to this restriction.

All articles are filed as A....... where the subsequent letters are an abbreviation of the article title. Picture-scripts are filed as SCOM.... (the first four letters indicating Story, COMMANDO series) followed by a three-letter abbreviation of the story title. And all books are filed under a three-letter abbreviation of the title followed by the chapter number, etc. Thus, this chapter is BOWC04, and the ProFiles are BOWPF01, etc. – in the BOOKS folder, BUSOWRIT sub-folder. (The Allison & Busby reports are filed as ABREP.. – the final two characters being numbers.)

Using this system means it never takes me long to find the computer file I want – unless I mis-filed it. Adapt the system to fit your own writing activities.

And it shouldn't need to be said, but I will anyway. Do make back-up copies of all your word processing files on removable floppy disks. Do it frequently – at the end of each day perhaps. If you take such precautions, you should never end up as one of those gloom-and-doom stories of authors losing their whole book when the computer or hard disk crashes.

Meetings

One day, you will be asked to visit your publisher or maybe a magazine editor. Something needs discussing. Don't be shy of such opportunities: it's great for all sides to put faces to names and voices – yours and theirs. Some such meetings will be very formal, others less so. Meetings over pub lunches are often the best – you get to know each other better. Just be sure you don't spill beer on the manuscript.

But there will always be a serious purpose to such meetings. The 'buyers' don't invite you in merely to see your face. They may want to adjust a synopsis, negotiate advances or print runs, or whatever, or invite you to write something different for them – a column perhaps. It is useful therefore if you can ascertain in advance the purpose of the meeting ... and prepare for it.

Before the meeting, make brief notes – the back of an envelope gives the right casual-yet-efficient impression – of the points you want to clarify. At the meeting, make even briefer – but careful – notes of what is agreed. Right at the start of the meeting too, take note of the names of all present: everyone likes being addressed by name. Immediately the meeting is over, and you're away, expand on your notes – while the events are still clear in your mind.

As soon as you get back to your desk, write briefly to your contact, or whoever called the meeting, recording your understanding of what was decided. (Write it as an expanded 'Thank-you' note if you don't want to appear over-pushy.) By getting your own version in early, you are recording your clear understanding; it may help whoever is writing formally to you. But of course, don't 'cook the books' – don't try to change what was decided, by falsely recording a slightly different result. You'll always get caught.

5

THE MERCHANDISE – YOUR MANUSCRIPT

As already discussed, it is important that a writer makes a good impression on editors and publishers. The first impression comes from the correspondence, the enquiry and, perhaps, the initial meetings. But – at the end of the day – what really counts is the actual merchandise: your manuscript. A business-like writer ensures that his/her submitted work is properly presented.

At the risk then of repeating what is well-known – and in defence, editors and publishers still receive much really badly presented material – there is generally only one correct way of presenting material for publication. (And the inclusion of that 'generally' is because some publishers may request different presentation – of which more later.)

Layout of typescript

Whether the manuscript is a novel or non-fiction book, a feature article or short story:

● It must be 'typed', not hand-written – and if produced using a word processor with a choice of fonts and sizes, then in a 'conventional' font and about the same size as typescript. I use 11-point Univers. (A 'conventional' font could include anything from a 'printed' look, such as Times New Roman, to a 'cleaner', *sans serif* font such as Univers – but NOT the more 'jokey' fonts.)

If a typewriter is used, it matters not whether the typeface/font is *pica* or *elite* (10 or 12 characters per inch.), so long as it is a conventional typeface, not mock-hand-writing or all capitals.

- It should be presented on white A4 (210 mm x 297 mm) paper of a 'reasonable' weight. (Paper thickness is measured by weight – the standard units are grams per square metre, gsm – and a paper of 80 gsm is about right. Over-weight paper may look/feel lavish, but its use will push up the postage costs, to no advantage. Conversely, thin, light-weight, bank paper will appear cheeseparing – and be hard to handle.

- It must be double-spaced – that is type a line, miss a line-space, not half a line-space – with wide margins on all four sides of the page. A left margin of 1.5 inches, a right margin of 1inch and top and bottom margins of 1.5 inches and 1 to 1.5 inches respectively are recommended. (Figure 5.1 shows a typical page layout.)

- It should have a consistent indent (say, five spaces, or 0.5 inch) at the start of every paragraph ... except the first in each article, short story, or chapter and the first beneath any internal headings, which should not be indented at all. (Note the indents on each 'ordinary' paragraph in this book and those immediately following headings.)

- It should not have blank line-spaces between paragraphs – as is common in blocked, non-indented, business letters. (Extra line-spaces make it more difficult for editors to estimate the overall number of words.) If you are including headings though, leave a blank line above and below each of these; some publishers prefer two or more line-spaces above a heading and one line below.

- It should include a means of page and overall identification on each page. In word processor terms, a 'header' – a part-line in the top right corner of the page, within the top margin. This should be something like, 'Title/Writer/Page number'. The full title is unnecessary: select a key-word from the title and use this. Similarly, just your surname.

Number the pages consecutively throughout the whole manuscript – DO NOT number the pages of individual chapters separately from 1. (Some writers give only title and name in the top right corner, numbering the pages centrally at the foot of the page. There's nothing wrong with this – but I think it's unnecessary and confusing. Best keep it all together – at top right.)

THE MERCHANDISE – YOUR MANUSCRIPT

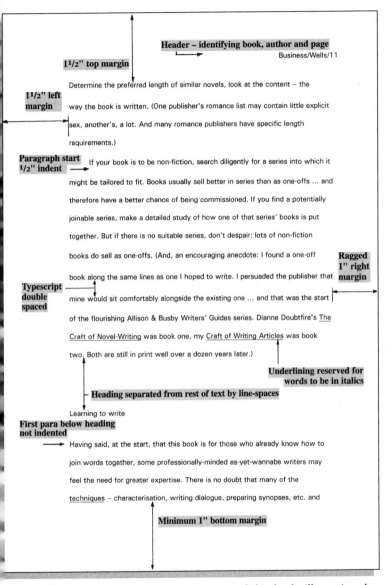

Figure 5.1: A sample page from the typescript of this book, illustrating the layout of the typed page. A virtually identical layout would be used for a story or article submitted to a magazine.

- Many editors and publishers prefer a manuscript to be typed 'ragged right' – that is, NOT 'right justified', as is now so easily done, using a standard word processor option. (Right justification – the neat and attractive ending of all lines precisely at the right margin – is achieved by the computer inserting additional spaces between words, to fill up the line. Then, when the editor/publisher comes to preparing the text for printing, it is not always clear which additional spaces are the author's intention and which the computer's.)

- Book manuscripts should be presented as a single 'bundle' – possibly with just an elastic band around all the pages, and/or in a paper-box or loose wallet – rather than chapter by chapter. (Personally though, I often paper-clip individual chapters; the clips are readily discardable. The really important thing is not to bind the pages, either in a loose-leaf binder or more impressively. Editors prefer dealing with a handful of loose pages – they're easier to cope with in the train ... or in bed.)

   Manuscripts for magazines are preferred paper-clipped or possibly stapled; never pinned – magazine editors are invariably haemophiliacs. (Or worried about how long it took for the prince to get round to the Sleeping Beauty?)

- There are two schools of thought regarding cover sheets for magazine submissions. Some writers do not provide them, but include their name and address and the number of words in the manuscript at the top of the first page. I always add a cover sheet, giving manuscript title, by-line, word count and my name and address. I think it looks better, more professional and – equally important – I'm told that some editors tear off the cover sheet, scrawl an agreed price on it and despatch it to the accounts section for payment. That could mean faster, or certainty of, payment. Whatever the result, the possibility is worth the sheet of paper.

   Whether you provide a cover sheet or not, for a manuscript submitted to a magazine, it's important to give the approximate word count somewhere on it. And don't be precise, even though your word processor tells you the exact wordage: the editor's usually only interested in a count to the nearest hundred words – so round it off, up or down.

A rough word count is also of use to a book publisher: for short-ish books (like this one) to the nearest 1,000 words is fine; for a blockbuster novel, maybe to the nearest 5,000 words. Base a book word count on the average number of words per *full* page of typescript times the number of typed pages. (That over-estimates the actual wordage, but is more useful for assessing book pages – which also have blank spaces at chapter starts and ends.)

● A final point about the submission of short manuscripts to magazines. Always enclose a stamped addressed envelope, correctly sized and stamped for the possible return of the submission. If this isn't included, the manuscript has a chance of being instantly binned.

After despatch

Once you have despatched your manuscript – whole book or maga-zine contribution – you must now do your best to forget it for a while. (Many – but regrettably not all – publishers will quickly acknowledge receipt. But that's all, for the time being.) You should not expect any (further) response for about a month. Many publish-ers – and some magazine editors – will take longer to respond.

Most professional writers will already have another idea, waiting on the back burner. Some authors take a brief rest before starting the next project, magazine writers can seldom afford to.

Assuming you have your next project lined up, now is the time to make a start on it. Or at least do some serious thinking about it. Working on something new will take your mind off the waiting.

New technology

Increasingly, magazine editors and publishers are asking for material to be supplied on computer disk. As already mentioned, there are certainly two – and possibly more – alternative ways of meeting that requirement: you can supply files prepared using the same word processor program as in the editorial/publishing office; or you can supply the material re-saved as an ASCII file, readable by any computer.

(I have frequently supplied book texts as ASCII files; the only problem, a recurring one, seems to be with paragraphing. The 'receiving' programmer has to convert your ASCII file back into a suitable word processor document – which means re-assembling the separate lines of the ASCII text into continuous prose. This conversion can – often, it seems – cause the deletion, or incorrect insertion, of paragraph-ends/starts: the 'Enter' key on your keyboard. Watch out for this when you get your proofs.)

Along with the text on disk, editors and publishers will always also want a 'hard copy' – the typescript. Some publishers will copy-edit a conventionally double-spaced typescript and return it to the author, complete with the disk ... and a request for the corrections to be made to the disk. There are two sides to this request: the author is doing extra work for the publisher, for free; but conversely, the author gets to see and accept all the corrections before the manuscript goes off for typesetting. It is, though, not unusual for a publisher to accept – or even specify, as one of mine does – a *single-spaced* hard copy typescript. If nothing else this saves on the author's postage bill.

There are other advantages to the author – particularly more technical authors with an interest in and awareness of book layout – in supplying work on disk. The detailed layout can be pre-agreed and incorporated in the preparation of the manuscript. (When preparing the material for my own, biennial *Magazine Writer's Handbook*, I write each magazine report to an exact page layout, based on font size, column width and lines per page. Thus, each report fills the page ... and there are no widows or orphans requiring last-minute correction.)

Multiple submissions

But let us revert, briefly, to the pre-submission, pre-contract stage of the book-writing business. You have written a novel, it's as good as you can make it, and you're desperately trying to find a publisher (or agent). It frequently takes two to three months for the manuscript to be sent off to a potentially suitable publisher, for it to be 'read' and commented on, and for the author to be told of its (likely) rejection. And then you read of agents offering their clients' books to several publishers at the same time and even holding an auction to determine the highest bidder. Can an individual author not do something similar?

Within reason, the answer nowadays is yes. A wannabe novelist need not hesitate to send the synopsis and first three sample chapters to more than one publisher at a time. (Twenty years ago, when publishing was an occupation for gentlemen, unconcerned with the grubby world of finance, multiple submissions were decidedly 'not the done thing, old chap'. Today, the accountants are in charge.)

The one qualification to the plan to submit a manuscript simultaneously to several publishers is that each should be made aware that other (not necessarily named) publishers are also being offered the book. And, equally important: as soon as one publisher makes a firm offer, the others should be told, to save them wasting further time.

The same approach – with the same 'awareness' qualification – could be adopted with a non-fiction book proposal, but there never seems to me to be that much need. A novel will usually be finished before it is offered to publishers; a non-fiction book should not proceed far beyond synopsis stage until publication is agreed.

You should NOT adopt a multiple submission approach when dealing with magazine editors – neither for articles nor for short stories.

In the publisher's office

Your finished book has been accepted: what happens now? (And this section relates only to books – a writer seldom gets a second look at work submitted to a magazine ... before publication. One or two up-market magazines *do* give the writer the opportunity of checking proofs, but this is most unusual.)

Within the publisher's office your manuscript will be carefully read by one or more editors: a commissioning editor and a copy editor – but the two roles are often merged. Is it all consistent – and understandable; is it 'plotty' enough; is it 'right' for the target readership? Have you made any spelling or grammatical errors? Overall, does the text conform to 'house style'?

House style can be little more than requiring e.g., 'ise' rather than 'ize' spelling, TV rather than T.V., double quote-marks for dialogue rather than single, and OK rather than okay. It can though extend to a whole bookful of instructions for a non-fiction (usually academic) author. For one recent book I was required to leave a double space after a full stop – rather than my usual single space.

In nearly all cases, once a book has been copy-edited, the manu-script will be sent back – with a number of queries – to the author: for checking and agreeing corrections or for amending where nec-essary. In most cases, changes made by copy-editors are sensible and should be adopted/agreed. Authors are not infallible – often far from it – and the copy-edit check can be extremely valuable in pre-serving their good name. (I once mis-spelled *accommodate* throughout an entire book. I can now spell it correctly. I've also, I think, now learned how to use a colon correctly. Thanks, ladies. I've never had a male copy editor.) But copy editors are not infallible either, and can be insensitive – or just plain lacking in understand-ing of a difficult (non-fiction) subject. The author/copy-editor relationship is often of a love/hate nature.

Whether the queries are few or legion, it pays to take note of all the changes made by the copy editor. It's a good way of learning YOUR trade.

At the copy-editing stage, the author is sometimes asked to key the agreed changes into the computer file(s) and return them, so that the final agreed text can go to typesetting. There is a case for the author being paid extra for doing this re-keying. It was never done by the authors in days gone by. Most publishers will reject such a suggestion though – the financial side of publishing is under considerable pressure. If you do key in the agreed corrections yourself, at least you are sure that the material which goes for typesetting – direct from disk – is correct. There are few later opportunities for errors to slip in.

Eventually, a batch of page proofs will land on your doorstep. Irrespective of what your contract (*see* Chapter 7) may say about the time within which you must clear proofs, these will always be wanted back yesterday. And this is the time when your book is actually beginning to take shape – so, as a business-like author you won't want to delay its progress.

Burn the midnight oil going through your proofs. Clear them as quickly as possible. And DON'T assume that this is an opportunity for you to make changes to your original text. It isn't – and if you do, it'll cost you. Read your contract. Proofs are for the correction of basically non-authorial errors – printers' cock-ups.

Be prepared to accept the odd sentence or paragraph where perhaps you don't like the way the editor has changed your words – unless it is a really disastrous mistake. You will probably be the only person to notice the awkward phraseology. Don't act like a *prima donna* over your text.

Magazine publication

Just as studying copy editors' changes is an excellent way of learning grammar and clear expression, so too is comparing your published magazine articles and short stories with your original typescript.

Pay particular attention to any changes the magazine editor has made: the shortening of your sentences and/or paragraphs, maybe the linking together of over-short paras, the deletion of waffly explanations or descriptions, the deletion or re-phrasing of excessive use of 'he/she said'. Whether or not you agree with the editorial changes, that's the way the editor likes it. If you want to continue selling more work, always provide what the editor wants.

6

KEEPING RECORDS – AND ACCOUNTS

Being business-like is much more than turning out competent, well-presented work though. It also entails knowing exactly what you're up to, what you're doing, who you're sending work out to – and when, and what payments you are due (and getting). Above all, the business of writing is about being *sensible* with and about money. If you're in business, your earnings – or, more correctly, your profits – are the measure of your success.

Before getting into details about financial matters though, the more mundane task of simply keeping tags on your work. The business-like writer has to keep records.

Records of submissions

If you haven't already started keeping records of every piece of work that you submit to magazine editors ... start immediately. (We'll come on to keeping records of work being offered to book publishers later.) Let's think first about the reason for keeping such records. There are several good reasons.

● You want to know what work you've submitted where – and the date. If you don't get a response within say a month, you might well wish to enquire, very gently, as to the fate of your submission.
● You want to know, in say six months time, when considering where next to submit a so far unsuccessful short story, where you have already offered it. It looks most unprofessional to submit the same, already-rejected, story again.

- Along much the same lines, you want to know where an article *idea* has been rejected before you offer a brand-new article *based on a similar idea* to the previously uninterested editor.
- Because of the often long periods between submission, acceptance, publication and payment, you want to know what accepted work has still to be published – and has not yet been paid for.
- Because each magazine (and editor) is individual, you need to build up information on their consideration, acceptance and payment procedures: how long they usually take to respond, publish and pay.
- I believe it's also useful – and certainly interesting – to know how many pieces of work you are turning out per year ... and your success rate.

All of the above benefits can be yours by maintaining one fairly simple table. Before I had a computer, my table was in writing. Nowadays, it's on the computer. Either way is perfectly reasonable – indeed, I possibly kept a better watch on my records when doing it manually.

> Be professional with queries, submissions, and invoicing. Always keep records of contacts, work submitted, accepted or rejected, and past, present and future work. If you don't, and are working concurrently on projects, it's easy to forget about queries and submissions and to forget when you should have been paid.
>
> Louise Cahill

I suggest the table should be on a single A4 sheet (or equivalent) with each piece of work having its own line; its progress, etc., being charted within a number of across-the-page columns with the following headings.

- **Item number** (I number each piece of magazine work throughout the year – and find it useful to identify the year too. Thus 012 will represent the financial year 2001-02, followed by a two-digit number – I haven't yet written more than 99 short pieces [plus books] in a single year. The final number is thus 01233, being the 33rd piece of work sent out in that year.)

- **Computer file name** (Despite the ability of Windows 95 to accommodate longer file names, I keep to the old MS-DOS practice of no-more-than-eight-character file-names. I differentiate between fiction and articles by the first letter – A for article, QA for article query/outline, S for story/fiction – followed by a possibly abbreviated keyword from the title. Thus, ATAGS is an article about keeping tags on magazine submissions. Similarly, SWKRAG is one of a series of short stories about my WizKid character and, this time, a clothes (rags) shop.)
- Abbreviated title – in case the computer file name is insufficient identification.
- **Length and illustrations** (Number of words, or, in the case of picture-scripts, number of frames, plus the number of submitted illustrations. Thus for an article, 1200/2 means a 1200-word article with two accompanying pictures. And 28f means a 28-frame picture-script.)
- **Magazine to which submitted.**
- **Date submitted** (I convert all dates into a consistent 6-figure number. Thus 25 March 1999 is listed as 250399.)
- **Decision** (A for accepted, R for rejected.)
- **Decision date.**
- **Magazine's publication date.**
- **Payment** (Once I know how much I am to be paid, I enter the figure within a bracket. When I get the money, I delete the bracket. This is easy on a computer; when listing manually, I entered the expected figure in pencil and inked over it when paid.)
- **Payment date** (Useful for my future reference – to know how long I should expect to wait for payment.)
- **A final blank column allows for comments** You have to write small to get all these columns across a single A4 sheet anyway, so it's a narrow column. But with the possibility of selling second rights in short stories, this column is a good place for a cross-reference to a second entry.

On those occasions when something is rejected – yes, no matter how experienced you are, you'll still get rejections – I use the last four columns to note if and where I re-submit it. But with work usually being tailored to just one specific market, this is not much used nowadays.

Book offers

It is just as important to keep tags on your book submissions. If, like me, you write mostly non-fiction, you will think up and offer around quite a number of book proposals. (As we all know, you have to kiss a whole lot of frogs before you find a real prince. For kisses, read non-fiction book proposals; for princes read publishers.) Just as with shorter works, you don't want to offer anything twice to the same publisher – so, once again there is a need to keep records.

These records can be simpler than that recommended above for magazine submissions. Even if you are really prolific, you are unlikely to come up with as many book proposals as articles. And with fiction, where the output of complete novels is usually smaller, the need is the same – merely less of a task.

I have not always kept records of book idea submissions. And, because it can sometimes take a year or so to get a non-fiction book 'off the ground', I once inadvertently re-submitted a book proposal to a publisher who had already turned it down. I don't think the publisher actually recognised it, but he still re-rejected it. I vowed though, never to let this happen again: I don't like egg on my face.

So ... if you're not yet keeping record of where you're offering your books, start now.

My current practice is merely to head a page (a simulated page within a computer file) with the working title of a non-fiction book idea and beneath that, tabulate details under the following headings, with a fresh line for each publisher.

- Publisher to whom the book idea is offered
- Date proposal [synopsis and 'sales pitch'] posted
- Publisher's reply date
- Publisher's decision

Once a publisher is 'hooked', the book idea becomes a working project – and I no longer need to keep tags on where it's at. (Merely on progress, for which, refer back to word budgets and daily output figures – *see* Chapter 1. I also keep a writing diary, recording what I am working on and when.) A similar record of submissions would be appropriate for the synopses and early chapters of a novel.

Chasing payments

At some time or other, most writers find themselves waiting – and waiting – for payment. My own experience of late payments suggests that this is more often with magazines than with book publishers, but publishers tend to pay rather late 'by right' (look at your Agreement). Magazines are more likely to be run on a shoestring – which usually leads to late payment. So, what should you do?

First, you need to know the payment system adopted by the magazine or publisher. Does the magazine pay on acceptance or – more likely – on publication? What, exactly, do they mean by 'on publication'? It's most unlikely that they will issue the payment cheques on the actual day of publication: more likely, they will be issued monthly, at the end of the month. The magazine will not like being chivvied for payment before their end-of-month payment day. Some magazines pay at the end of one (and occasionally two) month(s) *after* publication. Find out – by tactful telephone enquiry – before you blow your top.

Some magazines and publishers, and many newspapers, only pay (some time) after receipt of a specific invoice. Again, you need to know their system and abide by it. (Refer back to Figure 2.1, page 36, for an example of one way of preparing an invoice.)

It often helps, particularly if you are selling frequently to one magazine, to back up your invoice(s) by regular monthly statements of account – recording payments made and payments (over)due. (Again, *see* Figure 2.1 for an example of a typical statement.)

If, despite invoices and statements – which are usually effective – you are still waiting for a well-overdue payment, you should:

- write a polite but firm letter to the editor of the guilty magazine – but be prepared thereby to rule yourself out of further work for this market;
- stop submitting work to this market, forthwith; and
- if all else fails, apply to the Small Claims Court for payment. You won't need legal assistance in this – it's quite simple and painless.

Find your nearest County Court (from the phone book); ask for three copies (one for you, two for the court – of which, one to be sent to the defendant) of form N1, the Default Summons Form; complete and return the (simple) forms – with the court fee. The fee is 10 per cent of the amount claimed – and is added to your claim if you 'win'. The case will be heard by a district judge, in private – no other lawyers – and is very informal. If the judge finds in your favour, the defendant (the magazine) will often settle immediately. If the defendant still doesn't pay up, further action becomes expensive; you will have to consider abandoning the claim and writing off the debt.

Are you profitable?

As well as recording payments – as mentioned above in the section about magazine submissions – you also need to record the 'other side' ... your expenses. As Mr Micawber said, '… income twenty pounds, ... expenditure twenty pounds nought and six, result misery.'

If your writing is costing you more than you're earning, you're not in business, it's an indulgence. (I suppose you might believe that you are 'investing' your money now in order to make a sizeable profit when you eventually sell your great work. If so, make sure you can at least convince yourself.) But whether it's meant to be a real business, or 'jam tomorrow', if you don't keep records of both your writing earnings and writing expenses, you won't know whether there's any jam at all.

Income tax

You don't only need to keep financial records for your own benefit. As soon as you earn anything, you become liable for Income tax on that amount. So the tax man too will require you to keep records.

A writer's financial records need not – at least until you get into the Big League – be very complex or sophisticated. Even the tax man doesn't ask for detailed accounts of a writer's income if it is less than a few thousand pounds a year. (There is little point in quoting specific figures for the tax requirements as these are liable to change from year to year.)

Initially, it may be sufficient merely to record all expenses and all receipts. A simple cash book could suffice: record income on one half of a double-page spread, and all items of day-to-day expenditure on the other. Wherever possible, keep your receipts. There are advantages – mainly of simplicity – in adopting the standard government financial year, commencing 6 April each year, for your own accounts. When you start, your most significant running expense is likely to be postage costs, but don't forget to also include the cost of outgoing phone calls.

Assuming that, before long, at least, you will invest in a computer and printer, you should definitely record such an expense. Once your writing is earning, you can set part of the capital cost against each year's income, for tax purposes.

(Currently, 25 per cent of the residual cost can be set against income each year. That is, if the equipment cost £1,000, £250 can be treated as an expense in the first year, leaving £750 residual cost. In the second year, 25 per cent of the £750 is an allowable expense – that is £187.50, leaving a residue for the following year of £562.50. If you then buy another piece of relevant equipment, the full cost of that can be added to the current residual figure – and 25 per cent of the new *total* claimed as an expense. As an example, during the year when the residual figure was £562.50, if a fax machine was bought for an arithmetically convenient £237.50, the new residue would be £800 of which 25 per cent, £200, would be allowable as an expense.)

Be sure to include all relevant expenditure in your accounts. It's easy to forget the packet of paper-clips, the extra ream of paper, the phone call to a contact to confirm a date or name. All these are reasonable expenses to set against your modest writing income – both for your own check on profitability and for tax purposes.

As your writing income – and expenditure – rises, as it should, you will probably find it helpful to break it down beyond the simple income or expense. I use a ready-ruled cash analysis book with double-page spreads allowing me to break down and summarise the figures more usefully for the tax man.

I use a double-page spread each month. After columns for the date and a description of the expenditure or income, the first two columns are the same as in any simple accounts – total income and total expenditure. In subsequent columns I further separate out the expenditure into such elements as postage, stationery, research, travel, phone/fax costs, etc. These subsequent columns are a split-up repetition of the figures in the total expenditure column. Apart from showing me where my money is actually going, this segregation is useful when I prepare my end-of-year balance sheet for submission to the tax inspector.

Because the income entries are far fewer, I merely indicate their source categories – by an initial letter – in a narrow, single column alongside the initial entry. (I separate out income sources into **A**rticles, **B**ooks, **L**ecture fees, **S**ale of books, **P**icture-scripts and **R**eaders' reports for publishers.)

Other sources of income

Once you have written your first book – and anyone in the business of writing will eventually, if not sooner, get round to writing a book – it should be registered for Public Lending Right (PLR).

Each time a book is borrowed from any UK public library, that loan is recorded – and the author is eligible to receive a small payment. (In practice, book-borrowings are recorded at a changing sample of UK libraries and the national total is grossed up from the sample figures.) The payment to the author is made annually and is currently about two pence per loan – it varies from year to year. But if your book is not registered with the PLR office, you won't be paid.

When your first – and every subsequent – book is published, and not before, it should be registered with the Public Lending Right Office, Bayheath House, Prince Regent Street, Stockton-on-Tees TS18 1DF. Initially, ask for a registration form. The PLR year runs from 1 July to 30 June; a notification of earnings is sent out at around the end of the year, and payments are usually made during the following February. Once you have more than one book registered, the earnings of all your books are added together for payment. No author can (currently) be paid more than £6,000 and earnings of less than £5 are similarly not paid.

PLR is funded by central government (in 1996/7 the provision was £5,000,000); there are nearly 26,000 registered authors and nearly ten times that many books. About 60 per cent of registered authors earn less than £100 a year from PLR (and a further 14 per cent – including me – less than £500), but no matter how little, it is well worth registering for – it's extra money.

A further source of 'unexpected' income is the Authors' Licensing and Collecting Society Ltd (ALCS). The ALCS collects copyright and other fees which authors cannot readily collect themselves and makes annual distributions to members. Much of their revenue comes from photocopying licenses in the UK (collected by their associated organisation, the Copyright Licensing Agency Ltd [CLA]) and from the PLR schemes in other countries. Membership of the ALCS is only a few pounds per year – and is free to members of the Society of Authors or the Writers' Guild of Great Britain. Book titles have to be separately registered with the ALCS – details from ALCS, 74 New Oxford Street, London WC1A 1EF.

Other forms of tax

It is not difficult to remember that you have to pay income tax on your writing earnings. If you're a spare-time writer, you know that you already pay PAYE on your earnings at the day job. Income tax is a fact of life.

It is easier to forget about the other UK income-related tax – the National Insurance contribution.

All self-employed persons are liable to pay Class 2 NI contributions; these are, currently, a few pounds, payable weekly. (And that's not all: Class 2 NI contributions suffice only for a specified level of earnings. If your self-employed writing earnings exceed the specified level, you will also be liable for Class 4 NI contributions – which are a percentage of all earnings above the specified level.) And I apologise for my deliberate numerical vagueness. There is no point in quoting either the weekly NI contributions or the earnings level above which Class 4 contributions are payable – they are subject to annual changes by the Chancellor of the Exchequer.

You may think your writing earnings are too small, too insignificant, to be 'eligible' for National Insurance (NI) contributions – and you may be right. But you need formally to establish this exception from liability.

There are two basic grounds for exception from self-employed National Insurance contributions:

1. If you are a woman aged over 60 or a man over 65, you don't have to pay any NI contributions at all.
2. If your self-employed writing earnings are under a couple-of-thousand-odd pounds per year (again, the figure is subject to change) you can apply for a Small Earnings Exception certificate. If your earnings are even smaller – less than about a thousand a year (again, changeable) – *you must still apply* for exception from liability for Class 2 contributions, but you won't be issued with a certificate. You will merely be advised that your earnings are too small for payment of contributions. This non-certificated advice – which is particularly relevant to many spare-time writers – remains valid until your circumstances change: you do not need to renew it. But you do need to be aware of – and watch out for the 'approach' of – the non-certificated exception level.

If you are below the limiting age and if you haven't already, elsewhere, worked up a full number of years' contributions, it is almost certainly worth opting to pay the basic Class 2 contributions voluntarily. This will bolster up your now imminent state pension.

One further point that is unlikely to bother many writers: there is a maximum level of NI contribution – currently around £30 per week.

In order to have realistic figures to replace the vague ones above, ask at your local DSS office (listed under Contributions Agency in your telephone directory) for the following leaflets.

- FB 30   Self-employed?
- NI 27A NI for people with small earnings from self-employment
- NI 41   NI guide for the self-employed

Value Added tax (VAT) is another tax of which the business-like self-employed writer should be aware. Few 'ordinary' writers though will earn sufficient to entail their *having* to register for VAT and the advantages of VAT-registration – mainly being able to reclaim VAT on purchases – are not large enough to warrant 'voluntary' registration. (The level at which VAT registration is compulsory is currently a 'total throughput of money' of about £50,000 per year. If that's you, you don't need this book – get yourself an accountant.)

We're none of us getting younger

Having already mentioned the state pension, one last point about our approaching old age. (And if you're only in your twenties or thirties, be warned – you're still getting older all the time. It pays to think about pensions. Even now. The sooner you start, the more you – eventually – get.) You can buy yourself a self-employed pension, even if your writing earnings are relatively small.

Present tax regulations permit some pension contributions to be set against taxable self-employed earnings. This is clearly advantageous in that the contributions – a form of savings – are therefore tax-free. The proportion of your earnings that can be diverted into a pension fund is dependent on your age: the older you get, the more of your writing earnings you can use to buy a pension. (Once again, tax-free allowances are subject to annual changes: enquire from your local tax office for current regulations.)

And, because a writer's earnings tend to fluctuate, you should choose a life assurance company that will accept variable annual lump sum payments rather than regular monthly contributions as preferred by many self-employed people (such as those in the building trade). There is no reason why you shouldn't pay your annual contribution to a different assurance company each year. I did, on the advice of my bank – and now wish I hadn't. I have several irritatingly tiny pensions rather than one large(r) one.

Having purchased a self-employed pension, you can opt to start drawing it at any age between, usually, 50 and 75. A proportion of the accumulated pension fund can then – when you start to draw it – be withdrawn as a tax-free lump sum. The pension payments themselves will of course be taxable.

Seek financial advice before buying a personal pension – and not just from one company-tied adviser.

7

THE 'SMALL PRINT'

This sentence, this paragraph, this chapter, this book is copyright. There is however no need for that to be specified.

Copyright

Whatever I write, whatever I commit to paper (or save electronically, as on a computer disk), is automatically and immediately protected by copyright. There is no need for me to register it or deposit a copy in some remote and stuffy archive. (Nor to place a dated copy in a sealed envelope and deposit that with a bank or solicitor.) Anyone who makes an exact copy of this paragraph is infringing my copyright. And that copyright remains effective for 70years after my death – which I trust is not imminent.

And that, in a nutshell, is what copyright is all about. The copyright is mine. I can assign it – i.e. transfer the right to another – wherever I wish.

But let me expand on the basics. The copyright applies to the way in which I have expressed the above statements – not to the statements themselves, which are facts. There is no copyright in facts. There is no copyright in ideas. (There is no copyright in titles, either – but that's basically because they are too short.) The copyright, in all cases, is in how the facts and/or ideas are expressed. If you wish, you can write a piece about copyright, making all the same points as I am doing here – as long as you express them *in your own way*.

Plagiarism is more complicated. If someone uses the original research of another, rephrases the descriptions, etc., and *passes the original work off as his own*, that is plagiarism. The same principle could apply to the detailed storyline of a novel – but not to the basic plot idea, of which there are supposedly only a certain number.

Every time a writer offers a piece of work to a magazine editor or book publisher, he or she is offering the RIGHT to publish it – an assignment of the copyright.

Serial rights

When a writer offers a feature article or short story to a magazine editor, he/she is offering First British Serial Rights, often abbreviated to FBSR. With articles, the offer of FBSR is usually taken for granted – it need not be specified. With short stories, because there are opportunities to sell other than those specific rights, it is customary to specify the rights offered.

But first, an explanation of the terminology. First British Serial Rights mean ... just that. You are offering the First (i.e. not second or ...) Right (i.e. an assignment of the copyright) of Serial publication (i.e. in a magazine which appears serially – in other words, daily, weekly, monthly, etc. – as opposed to the one-off publication of a book) in a British (as opposed to American, Scandiwegian, or Ethiopian) magazine. You cannot offer *First British* rights if your work has already been published in Britain, even if only in a parish or small press magazine, and irrespective of whether or not it was paid for. You can though, offer First Danish rights, for instance, even if the British publication in which it has already appeared was world-renowned, and a high payer. You can offer an already British-published short story for inclusion in a British anthology, because only *Serial* (rather than Book) Rights have previously been released.

When offering a short story to a magazine, you should indicate the rights you are offering on the story's cover sheet – 'FBSR offered'. If offering second or non-Serial rights, mention should be made of the circumstances of the previous publication. (Many British magazines will not object to considering a story that has previously appeared in a small press magazine or been broadcast on the radio – as long as they are aware of what they're getting.)

While a short story is written as a stand-alone entity – and would not be rewritten to suit the style of different magazines – an article is more market-oriented. You could write up a single set of facts in different styles for different magazines. For that reason, there is little point in indicating that you are offering FBSR in your article: that is taken for granted.

There is virtually no market for Second British Serial Rights in an article – and what there is, is low-paying. More important, having sold the article once, there is nothing to stop the business-like writer from writing up the same set of facts again, with a *different slant*, in a *different style*, for a different magazine. You can again offer a legitimate FBSR.

(A magazine editor may sometimes require something other than FBSR. I have occasionally been asked to sign a payment receipt form releasing Full World Rights or All Rights For All Purposes. Because I am merely selling the copyright in the *form of words* used in that magazine-specific piece of writing, this never bothers me. I would not expect to sell the *identical* article again – and there is nothing to stop me from rewriting the facts and re-selling as FBSR.)

Book rights

When you submit your book manuscript to a publisher you are offering to assign the copyright to him for a period of time and in respect of a whole variety of possible uses – in exchange for payment – on which more, below. You are not (usually, and you should avoid doing so as far as possible) surrendering your copyright. You may, on occasions, and in specific circumstances, be expected to surrender your copyright, but be very careful. (Some publishers of children's non-fiction require the surrender of copyright: the author works for a flat fee. If you want to work in this field, you may have to accept the conditions.)

Take care though – when you offer/sell a short piece to a magazine, the situation is fairly standard: your work will be used once in the magazine. Unless you have sold more than First Rights your work will appear in print, you'll be paid (eventually) – and that'll be that. When dealing with publishers there are more rights involved than just book publication. Unless you negotiate a variation in your contract – and in some cases you definitely should – the publisher will cheerfully expect to be assigned:

● hardback, trade paperback and mass market paperback book rights;
● rights in other countries – American and other foreign language publication;
● film, TV and radio rights;
● electronic system rights – CD-ROMs and possibly use on the Internet;
● audio-book rights;
● rights in talking and Braille books for the blind.

In some cases, the publisher is the best person to take charge of these other rights. Much depends on the type of book. If your book is a potentially best-selling novel, you will do best to have an agent looking after your interests before you complete the contract-signing stage; the agent will almost certainly retain control of several of the extra rights. If we are talking about a non-fiction 'How-to' book aimed mainly at a British market – like this one – then few of the extra rights are of mega-value and may safely be entrusted to the publisher.

If you are negotiating the contract for your first book without the assistance of a guiding agent, you would be very wise to seek assistance from the Society of Authors. You can become a member as soon as you are at the negotiating stage and they offer excellent specialist legal advice. For details of the Society, *see* Appendix 2. DO NOT consult your local High Street solicitor about a publisher's contract: this is a specialist field of which many solicitors understand little.

The Publisher's Agreement

But we are getting ahead of ourselves. We have offered our work to a publisher and, understanding about copyright, we now know what we are offering. Having gone through the tortures of our 'baby' being rejected again and again, someone has at last said they like it. They would like to publish it. You have met and talked about how they will handle your offspring. And now a draft Agreement has landed on your door-mat.

It may not say it's a draft Agreement but you can take it as such. Publishers don't *like* variations to their supposedly standard Agreement, but if you ask for something sensible and realistic – and are firm about it – you'll often get the changes you wish.

The Agreement (or contract) will be a multi-page legal document, setting out the responsibilities and commitments of the two parties involved – the Publisher and the Author (you!).

There is no such thing as a totally standard Agreement – different publishers use different forms – but let me take you through one of mine, section by section. Yours will be much the same.

The work
This section identifies the author – as being the other party to the Agreement – and the book (by tentative/working title) and its extent (approximate overall length).

No problems – just facts.

Territory
This section clarifies the geographical territory for which the Author assigns the copyright to the Publisher. It will usually be either English-speaking countries, the same less specific areas (such as America), or the World.

No problems – but possibly important.

Author's warranties
Here, the Author is required to confirm that the work is original, accurate, and his/hers to sell. The Author is also expected to confirm that the work is not libellous, obscene, blasphemous, etc.

Hopefully, no problems here.

The publisher's undertaking
Here, the Publisher specifies when – subject to matters outside their control – the book will be published and guarantees that it will be

professionally produced. It also states that advances and royalties *will* be paid, in accordance with a later clause in the Agreement.

You should watch out for an over-long delay between manuscript delivery and book publication – 12 months is a fair average.

Delivery of typescript
Having been agreed with the Author, a delivery date for the typescript is specified. The format and number of copies of the typescript, supplementary computer disk, illustrations, etc., is specified. The Publisher also agrees to take good care of the typescript.

Once again, no problems – but do be realistic when pre-agreeing a delivery date for your typescript: I always calculate how long I shall need and then add on at least a month for contingencies. If you deliver early (but not too early) the Publisher will bless you; late and you'll be in the dog-house, with the (remote) possibility of the Publisher cancelling the Agreement, as would be their right.

Proofs, etc
The Author undertakes to check the proofs of his/her book within a specified short period; the Publisher warns that the Author will be charged with the cost of excessive alterations not due to printers' errors. The Publisher warns the Author that should there be a market for a new edition, this will be expected – for further remuneration.

All straightforward, but be warned: only a few author's changes are needed to run up a large typesetting bill. If this exceeds around 10 to 12 per cent (specified in the Agreement) of the original total typesetting bill, it will be charged to the Author.

Remember, PROOFS ARE FOR CORRECTION, NOT FOR REWRITING.

Copyright notice
The Publisher confirms that the standard copyright notice and the identification/assertion of the Author's moral right, will be printed in each edition of the book. There is also agreement about how any copyright infringement will be dealt with.

No problems here – the Publisher will usually take care of this.

Publisher's publication intentions

This is a clause which is not in all contracts – and in my case, while included, is not formally part of the contract – but it is helpful. The Publisher specifies the form – hardback, trade paperback or mass-market paperback – in which he intends to publish, the expected retail price and the likely size of the initial print run. Some publishers are exceedingly 'cagey' about the size of their first print runs. The figure is potentially of use – in checking the 'fairness' of the advance, see below.

Licence period

This specifies the period of time for which the Author licenses the Publisher to publish the Work. (Often, but potentially negotiable, for the duration of the copyright period – i.e. until 70 years after the Author's death.) The right to terminate the licence depends, basically, on the Publisher keeping the Work in print.

In most cases, this is not a particularly contentious section of the Agreement: if a book's in print and selling, there will seldom be a need to terminate the licence. (But see also Termination, below.)

Royalties and advances

The interesting bit. A royalty is a percentage of the book's (usually retail) price which is paid to the Author. It is 'fairly standard' for a publisher to pay 10 per cent royalty for hardback sales, 7 to 8 per cent for trade paperback sales and sometimes a considerably smaller percentage for mass-market paperback sales – in each case, on the list price. In each case, the royalty rates may increase after the sale of a number of copies of the book. These 'royalty jumps' are at specified but negotiable points – possibly 3,000 hardback sales, 10,000 trade paperback, and 20,000 mass-market paperback sales. The royalty jumps themselves are usually of 2.5 per cent.

There is a growing tendency for publishers to seek to pay royalties based on their net receipts, i.e., after allowing huge discounts to chain booksellers. There is nothing wrong with royalties based on receipts as long as the royalty percentages reflect the likely discounts. A 10 per cent royalty on a hardback selling at a retail price of £10 is £1. If a Publisher sells the book to a retailer at a not-at-all unusual 50 per cent discount, i.e. for £5, the royalty percentage based on receipts needs to be 20 per cent to earn the same £1. BEWARE!

An advance is an advance against future royalty earnings. In other words, once you've been paid an advance, this has to be 'earned out' or recouped by a Publisher before you will be paid any further royalties. For example: if you receive a £1,000 advance against 10 per cent royalties on a hardback book selling at £10, it takes the first 1,000 sales to recoup the advance. Only thereafter will you be paid further royalties.

An advance is usually paid in parts: on signing the Agreement, on delivery of the typescript, and the balance on publication. These parts might be 33/33/34 per cent or 50/25/25 per cent of the whole. The amount of the total advance and the tranches in which it is paid are fruitful areas for negotiation between Author and Publisher.

The overall size of the advance is not merely of financial importance to the Author – it can also reflect the Publisher's commitment to the Work. A large advance can mean a good publicity campaign. But negotiate with care: many smaller publishers are finding it hard to pay large advances – indeed, some are no longer offering advances at all.

Conventionally – and by long tradition in the publishing world – the size of a total advance is often about half the amount due from sale of the first print run. Thus, a £10 book on 10 per cent royalty would earn a total of £3,000 from an initial print run of 3,000 copies. An advance of half that, £1,500 would perhaps be considered fair. Some get much more – others less. (But when was life ever fair?)

Subsidiary rights
This section specifies the Author's share of the Publisher's income from overseas sales, audio-books, etc.

You might try negotiating for a larger percentage of, say, American sales. A literary agent will usually do better for you in this area – they know what to ask for.

Royalty statements
The Publisher specifies the annual dates when royalty statements will be delivered and payments made. Most publishers nowadays

pay twice a year, three months after the sales period being reported. A few publishers provide monthly sales statements (and payments) for the first six to twelve months after publication, six-monthly thereafter. But they are rare beasts.

No problems here, merely to be noted.

Remaindering

Many books sell reasonably well for their first year or so of life, sales tailing off dramatically thereafter. Depending on the numbers, publishers may wish to dispose of the unsold stocks at a very low 'remainder' price – around the unit production cost. This clause in an Agreement requires the Publisher to warn the Author of the intention to dispose of unsold stocks and give the Author the opportunity to buy copies at the 'remainder' price.

Straightforward section – and it's often worth buying some remaindered copies. (But don't go mad. If the Publisher can't sell them, can you?)

Author's copies

In this section the Publisher says how many free copies of the book he will give the Author, on publication. In years gone by, publishers were mean; they only gave the poor author half a dozen copies. Nowadays, 12 copies of a hardback and 20 of a paperback are more usual.

Termination of the Agreement

Here, the terms and condition are specified under which the Agreement may be terminated. From the Author's viewpoint, the most important provision of this section is for when the book is allowed to go out of print (OP). It is not uncommon for a publisher to decide that a book has 'run its course' and that further sales are unlikely to be at a commercially viable level. The publisher then lets the book go out of print. A good publisher notifies the author of this decision.

At that point the Author may – without distressing the Publisher – request the formal termination of the Agreement. The termination of the Agreement means that all the rights in the book which were the subject of the Agreement, revert to the Author.

One should ALWAYS revert rights to OP titles as soon as the terms of the contract permit. Over time there will be subsidiary income from foreign rights, translations, etc. Or even film rights which the original publisher should not be allowed to share unless they have kept the work in print. And often a successful later title will lead to the reprinting of OP work by a new and keener publisher if the rights in it are free. Keeping control of rights in OP titles is therefore a form of good housekeeping.

Jill Paton Walsh

I have never taken back the rights in a book – if the book has gone out of print then I would think it's probably past its best anyway.

Jacqueline Wilson

I would always ask for reversion of rights when a book is out of print and there's no intention of doing a new edition. Twice my agent has succeeded in selling new rights in books which the original publisher had finished with.

Jo Bannister

The reversion of the rights to the Author is important. Although the book is no longer commercially viable to the original publisher, it may be possible for the author to find another home for the book – another publisher willing to produce a new edition.

I have managed this on several occasions: McGraw-Hill published two editions of my book *How to Communicate*; they then notified me that they were not going to produce a third edition. I asked for, and got, the reversion of the rights. Not long after, I sold the book again, as a third edition under the new title of *Effective Communication* to Singapore publisher EPB.

More recently, Foulsham published a book of mine entitled *Make Money at Home*. Once the first print run had been sold, I was told that they did not envisage reprinting. Again, I asked for the rights to revert to me and resold the book: a second, higher-priced edition is now available from the new publishers, Management Books 2000 Ltd. Had I not reclaimed the rights, I could not have re-sold either book – and in each case there was a significant advance.

> I always have a clause in my contracts, allowing me to claim back rights in out-of-print books, if the publisher cannot guarantee to reprint within three months after receiving written notice from me. I have on occasions resold the reverted rights, sometimes, but not always, through an agent. I would recommend every writer to do the same.
>
> Diana Pullein-Thompson
>
> Always ask for the rights in a book to be reverted back to you, once it is out of print. It is then available for you or your agent to offer to a large-print publisher, for foreign rights, or for audio-cassettes, if these subsidiary rights haven't been sold already. This has worked successfully for me.
>
> Jean Saunders

And my *How to Write Non-Fiction Books* (Allison & Busby) is a major rewrite of *The Successful Author's Handbook* – originally published 15 years ago by Macmillan. I could not have rewritten it for Allison & Busby had Macmillan not finally decided to let it go out of print and released the rights back to me.

Disputes
This clause specifies the arrangements for settling otherwise irreconcilable disputes between Publisher and Author. I've never yet reached this stage. Few of us do.

Option for Author's new work
A publisher often invests time and money in building up the reputation of a new author – in the expectation of a string of future books. It is therefore reasonable for the Publisher to expect the Author to give him first refusal of the next book. This clause is usually qualified to refer to the next book 'of a similar nature'.

Legal interpretation
This specifies that the Agreement will be interpreted in accordance with the laws of ... usually, England and Wales, but my Singapore publisher specifies the laws of Singapore.

A straightforward clause of little normal import, unless you land up in court.

THE 'SMALL PRINT'

And that's what a pretty standard book contract is like. Don't be frightened by the look of your Agreement, it'll all work out all right – the Publisher will no doubt explain any particular clause that bothers you.

8

MORE MONEY FROM ...

Right at the start of this book, we looked at the opportunities for writers to diversify – to try something new. The field is vast, the opportunities legion. To be business-like – and make money – you must keep busy. But there are other ways to increase your income, without exploring the farther reaches of the field.

You can:

- Recycle your research – you should seldom write just one article; the same set of facts can frequently be re-used in a different way in a second market.
- Give talks about your writing experiences – and perhaps extend this to the regular, further education evening class teaching of writing.
- Sell copies of your books – either fiction or non-fiction; an ideal opportunity is after you've given a talk, or when lecturing.

In more detail now ...

Recycling research

Undoubtedly, the days of writing an article and circulating it around various magazines in the hope of someone accepting it are long gone. Feature articles have to be carefully targeted. Despite this fact, there are often a number of magazines with potential interest in what you've got to say. The business-like freelance writer seldom sells just one feature on a subject. Do the research, write the feature for the highest-paying market ... and then write another article, on the same subject but with a different slant, for another magazine.

An immediate example: I persuaded several of my fellow writers to help with my 'business' questions; their responses appear in the ProFiles and other comments throughout this book. I hope to incorporate some of these quotes (or their content) in an article for one or other of the writing magazines. That's recycled research. In past years I've collected much information about dragons; I haven't just written one article about dragons – I've written several. I hope to write more. (And a children's book too, if I'm lucky.)

Always keep your research material and notes. File the notes away carefully. One of these days you'll find a fresh use for them.

Talks and lectures

There are many organisations – not just writers' circles and conferences, but WI groups, men's lunch clubs, schools, even – who are always looking for someone interesting to come and talk to them. You can be that someone. And they pay their speakers.

But I can hear you saying, 'I couldn't stand up and give a talk. I'm much too nervous.' Forget it. You CAN do it. And, in time, you could even come to enjoy giving talks. Certainly, it's a stimulating experience. And don't worry about being nervous – we all are. A speaker who doesn't suffer at all from pre-talk nerves is probably no good: he's over-confident. The nerves disappear within a few moments of starting the talk, anyway. And 'How-to' lectures are usually easier than one-off 'social' talks – you don't have to make 'em laugh.

The best way to learn to give a talk or lecture is ... to do it. But let me suggest a few ways to make the first-time talk less of a nightmare and more of a success. A talk or lecture is a four-stage process:

- planning
- preparation
- practice
- presentation

Planning

First, think about the who, the what and the why of your proposed talk. Ascertain too, for how long you are expected to talk. It's embarrassing to give a 20-minute talk in a one-hour slot. And the other way round is even worse for the listeners.

To whom is the talk to be given? You will need to give a different talk to school-children than you would give to the local WI – and different again to a writers' conference. You need to think about the audience's likely awareness, age and interests. You also want to have a rough idea of the size of your audience – a talk to 100 people needs different preparation than one to half-a-dozen. (In some ways, it's harder to talk to a handful.)

What are you going to talk *about*? Sort out in your mind just what your subject is to be. Yes, your writing, but what aspect? Are you going to explain generally how you started, how you work (intravenous black coffee and wall-to-wall Radio 2 perhaps, like me), or the historical background to one of your novels, or specifically how to do something (work up a storyline, write a non-fiction book synopsis)? Be as specific as possible – it'll save you worrying later.

Why? What is the purpose of the talk? Maybe to inform or educate – or should it be to entertain? What do the 'paying customers' want? (If, like me, you don't feel you can manage an entertaining talk, make this clear before you accept the invitation to talk.)

Make sure you've got the where and when sorted out too. You MUST arrive early. Check on directions and parking spaces.

Preparation

You know what you are going to talk about and the level at which you are going to put it across. Now, in detail, what are you going to say? You need to collect your material, structure the talk (arrange the sequence in which you present the material) and make the notes from which you will speak.

Spend some time thinking about the points, the facts, the information that you need or want to include. List them – all – on a sheet of rough paper. Keep adding to them over a period of a few days if possible. Then rank them: sort them into essentials, desirables and make-weights (*musts*, *needs* and *wants*).

Next, consider the audience: you must give them the essentials, but it may well be best then to add in some of the lighter-weight material – anecdotes, jokes, even – to leaven the heavier facts. Think about it.

Now you have to structure your talk – to arrange the points in a logical sequence. This is not as difficult as it sounds. One way is to adopt the ageless 'three times three' approach: settle on three main aspects of your subject and put them across three times. (Outline the three things you are going to talk about, go through them in detail, and then remind the audience, briefly, of what you've told them.) And of course, you can make that four or even five things if that fits better – but audiences find it hard to take in too much at one sitting. Another structure is to offer 'Ten steps to ... Heaven' – list the steps and then explain them, one by one. And there is also – where appropriate – the 'historical' structure: go through your talk in the natural sequence of events.

Once the talk is structured, you can prepare your notes. Some people write their whole talk out verbatim: and when read to the audience, it sounds like just that – someone reading aloud. Unless you are a trained thespian or politician, a pre-written speech often comes across as really dull. I strongly recommend that you make only brief notes of what you wish to say and then speak from those notes. That way, the words will always come out fresh and alive – even if you do sometimes stumble over the delivery, no one will worry because it will come across as natural. (You will need more comprehensive notes for large audiences – but still only notes.)

My preference is to make my notes on small numbered cards; I punch a hole in the top left corner of each card and join them all together with a Treasury tag. That way, I can always find my way back if I drop them, or ...

Practice

You know what you are going to say; you have your notes from which to speak – but you still need to ensure that it will all *work*. DO NOT keep practising your talk until you know it all off by heart – that way, it will again come across as dull and lifeless. But you should go through it all once or twice; what pros call a 'stagger through'.

Give your talk to yourself – even in front of a mirror perhaps, if you want to practise gestures, etc. – and check that the material is sufficient to last out the allotted time. (If not, go back to your list of *musts*, *needs* and *wants* and add in some of the material you left out – or go searching elsewhere for more.) If you've got too much material in your notes, that's fine. You can trim it 'on the night' – for now, just identify the less essential items on your note-cards.

Presentation

So now you come to the moment of truth. Today you're giving your first talk. Arrive at the venue early – to make sure everything is under control (and that you've come on the right day). DON'T have a stiff drink before your talk – frequent hiccups ruin even the best presentations. You don't need Dutch courage, you've got your note-cards.

When the actual moment comes, stand up, look around, and start to speak. Those butterflies in your stomach will soon settle down and the adrenalin they have generated helps you to give a good talk. Initially, look directly at someone near the back of the audience. Your voice will carry where you look. (If not, you'll see the back-row person look puzzled: in which case, speak a trifle louder. If he/she looks really puzzled, don't worry – it's them that are in the wrong room, not you.) As you continue, change your view, look at someone else. Keep looking at different people – but each for some while, you're not watching tennis – and watch for their reactions. Are they nodding in agreement – or falling asleep? Do they at least smile at your weak jokes?

Work through your notes, keeping an eye on the clock (and trim the talk if it looks as though it is over-running: this is relatively easy when talking from notes – just say less about each, or skip one or two points) and don't move around nervously. Before you know it, the talk will be finished and you're on to questions – the easy bit.

There, now it's over, it wasn't too difficult or frightening was it?

Selling your own books

When you give a talk, if it's any good at all, your audience becomes interested in you and your work. They may wish to take away what is effectively a memento of the occasion; fired by your enthusiasm, they can often decide to buy a book which, in other circumstances, they might pass by. A business-like writer always has at least a few copies of his/her books available for sale.

Look at the section of your contract – and if you're at the stage of considering selling your books, you now have your own contract – which refers to *Author's copies*. It will usually say that the Author may purchase further copies of the book, 'for personal use' at a discount – usually 35 to 40 per cent. A blind eye is usually turned on the 'personal use' being to sell. Ask your publisher for a supply of your books.

If appropriate, mention or hold up a copy of your book during the course of your talk. There is a fine dividing line though, between modest pushiness and blatant salesmanship – try to stay on the right side.

There is also much to be said for letting your books be *seen* throughout your talk. Flat on the table beside you, they are insufficiently visible; at least stand them upright. If there is a suitable side table, display them on that. Some publishers produce – and, if asked, will let authors have – cardboard display stands that accommodate a dozen or so books.

Even if your publishers don't have display stands for *your* books, they may have them for their best-sellers. (Oh, the jealousy.) You can easily take someone else's display stand and cover it, to display your own name or message. That's what I've done.

Don't buy up too large a stock of your book(s) – you can always re-order if you need more. Delivery is usually very quick. Don't worry that your order is embarrassingly small – many bookshops order in ones and twos. I usually order in multiples of five. And you need to get a 'feel' for the way your books will sell: some will 'walk off the shelves', others will only go in ones and twos. Clearly, you need more stock of some than others; the price and relevance will undoubtedly have a bearing on this. (A paperback novel priced at £1.99 will sell more than a hardback at £14.99. A relevant 'How-to' book will – usually – sell more than a book of poems.)

A few more, practical, book-selling hints:

- Offer – tentatively – to sign the books – many buyers welcome this. (Some authors just sign, some add the buyer's name, others include a brief message. If you like the latter idea, it is worth sorting out in your mind a few suitable comments – there won't always be time to think while you're selling.)
- Take a small 'float' of change with you – you could lose a sale for the want of 50p change. (Buyers will willingly forego the odd penny on a £7.99 book – but not the two pounds.)
- Accept cheques – but make sure they're signed. (I accepted an unsigned one once and it took a week's following-up to get it signed by the highly embarrassed buyer.)
- Know how many copies of which book you have with you at any sales venue – this facilitates checking takings against stock balance. (I tabulate: book title, books brought, books left, *hence* books sold, sale price, *hence* takings per book – and total.)
- Keep financial records of book purchases and sales – and, to avoid confusion, make a separate note of any copies you give away. (Don't give too many copies away. Freebies are always popular.)

We have already mentioned, in the previous chapter, publishers' remaindering of no-longer-selling books. It is almost always worth your while – if you ever sell any copies of any of your books – to buy at least a few copies of your remaindered book(s). They will probably cost you less than a pound a copy, and you can often sell them for two or three times that. And even then, you will probably be selling at one-third the marked price. Joe Public adores a bargain. If you don't buy some copies, you will spit when you see your book advertised by the 'Bargain Book' specialists at the aforementioned one-third price.

An aside: Your own research buys should include remaindered copies of others' books on your specialism. The best 'Bargain Book' mail-order specialists are: Bibliophile Books, 5 Thomas Road, London E14 7BN (Tel: 0171-515 9222)

Self-publishing

The two concepts of retrieving your rights when your book is allowed to go out of print and buying up copies when it's remaindered leads nicely in to the subject of self-publishing. Contrary to your publisher's earlier experience, you may find that the copies of your book which you are selling at a bargain price are now moving very well. This is a moment for you to consider that book's future.

First, can you find another publisher to produce a new edition? If so, go for it. If not, maybe you could consider republishing it yourself. This could be a simple introduction to self-publishing. (The editing has been done for you. All you need to do is find a printer to reprint it for you – resetting the original pages – and put it in a fresh cover. Then ALL you have to do is sell it.)

Aside from new editions of a previously published book, publishing one's own work is a major step for any author.

Self-publishing is never an easy option. You, the author, have everything to do – and that 'everything' is an awful lot. A commercial publisher has, among other activities, to:

- make a judgement on the market viability of the book – to 'accept' it;
- arrange for the financing of the book – i.e, put up the money;
- check – and correct if necessary – the book's 'readability';
- edit the book – punctuation, grammar, spelling, consistency;
- design the layout – of pages and of the book as a whole (to fit to signatures);
- design the cover – and write the 'blurb' for the back;
- arrange for typesetting;
- check the proofs (an author's proof-reading alone is seldom sufficient);
- arrange for printing and binding – including fitting the cover;
- advertise/publicise the book;
- sell the book to booksellers;
- store and distribute the book copies;
- keep accounts.

ProFile 15

Writer/Publisher John Dawes – the pen-name of J A Davis, BSc Hons (London), BA (Open)

Biog In the 1960s, John Dawes wrote DIY articles in his spare time. In the late 1960s he worked on the development of private, commercial and public swimming pools, which led to his first book, *The Swimming Pool and The Garden* (Bartholomew, 1975) – which is still his own favourite. Further swimming pool books followed until, in the late 1980s, the takeover of his publishers and the belief that authors should have greater control over their own work, led him into self-publishing. His first self-published books were published jointly with the Institute of Swimming Pool Engineers; later books are under the John Dawes imprint. In 1993, with other technical writers in the Society of Authors, he founded – and for years chaired – the Author-Publisher Network.

Credits include *Design & Planning of Swimming Pools* (ISPE), *Take the Plunge* (English Tourist Board), *The Successful Indoor Swimming Pool* (John Dawes Publications, 1997).

Question What are your views on self-publishing?

This activity is a must for every author to explore. If production technology and book business is not understood by the author, how can he negotiate fair deals for all the work and imagination he has to conjure? Every kind of publication can be tried, assuming proper assessment has been carried through. Many writers who wish to be published will find that if they take the trouble to learn about the trade and the craft of writing *and* about publishing in doing their own project, the experience will demonstrate how the book world operates, and how they can fit or shape in that world. Self-published books entail twice or thrice the work, but can bring even more return. Join one of the self-help organisations listed in the writers' reference handbooks or read several of the good books about publishing some of your own projects.

These are time-consuming activities that will keep the author from doing what he/she is presumably best at – writing. And many are specialist activities, or activities that many authors will not feel competent to undertake, like the actual selling.

Self-publishing should not be condemned out of hand though. In bygone days, self-publishing was commonplace. Alexander Pope, Charles Dickens and Jane Austen contributed financially towards much of the cost of their books being published – and attracted significant sales income. Among many others, Rudyard Kipling, Beatrix Potter, Thomas Paine and Virginia Woolf were self-publishers at some stage in their careers. More recently, Jill Paton Walsh attracted much publicity when her self-published *Knowledge of Angels* was short-listed for the Booker prize.

> Self-publishing should be seen as a last resort. It is better to get your book published and distributed at someone else's risk and expense, and to have the process handled by experienced people with adequate staff and equipment, than to struggle with it yourself.
>
> These notes assume that the last resort has been reached, but you should not make that assumption too soon. The best prospects for self-publishing are books of local or minority interest for which you can identify the potential audience. The toughest ... are fiction, poetry and general interest books. Autobiographies are the hardest of all, unless you're a celebrity, in which case you will find a commercial publisher and won't even need to be able to write.
>
> The second rule, after 'Only do it as a last resort', is 'Don't risk more money than you can afford to lose.'
>
> The third rule is: 'Take all the advice you can get from anyone who knows what they're talking about.' This applies particularly when it comes to SELLING, which is by far the hardest part of all.
>
> (Extract from Some Notes on Self-publishing,
> © Jill Paton Walsh and John Rowe Townsend, 1996.)

Generally speaking, self-publishing is not a viable option for fiction. If a novel is worth publishing, you *ought* to be able to find a commercial publisher willing to take it on. Nor is it a viable option for *much* non-fiction.

Self-publishing is though, an option worth considering for highly specialist non-fiction and for solely local-interest non-fiction (e.g.

village guides or histories). Such non-fiction books have a narrow, well-defined market. A specialist book will sell to a specialist market, the whole of which can often be reached via trade or hobby magazines and organisations. Village guides, etc., can be sold through a small number of readily identifiable – and easily reached – local bookshops.

Self-publication is also a worthwhile – and often the only, even if still not commercially viable – option for poetry. Many poets have small booklets and one-off poem cards printed and successfully offer them for sale at readings. (Thanks, no doubt, to the 'personal appearance enthusiasm' mentioned above.)

If you have decided – after much soul-searching, several rejections by the commercial publishing world, and careful inspection of your bank balance – to proceed with self-publishing, the first step is perhaps to find a suitable printer.

Your friendly local printer is not necessarily the best person to go to. Nor is the big printer of mass-market paperbacks. Investigate the firms who nowadays specialise in small print-run book production. Don't get too carried away by the cheaper unit price of printing larger runs, it's better to print a small number and have to reprint, than to have 5,000 unwanted books cluttering up your spare bedroom.

Ask to see examples of similarly self-published books they have recently produced. Do they *look* self-published? (Many self-published books are obvious at a glance – wrong paper, poor page layout, badly-designed covers.) You want yours to look professional.

Check on the unit cost. From this, at about this stage, you need to determine the price at which you're going to sell your book. This will be a balance between what the market will bear and what will make you a reasonable profit. Commercial publishers are said to base their list price on unit production cost times five. Self-publishers should not work to a mark-up of less than three times: one for production, one-and-a-half for discount, distribution and marketing, and a half for themselves – author and profit.

Is the resultant cover price more than you think the book will sell for? Don't drop the price, go for it. You're probably wrong. And remember – bookshops will demand big discounts before they even put your book on the shelves. (Which is a plus point for the specialist book selling to a small, well-defined market by mail order.)

ProFile 16

Writer Peter Finch

Biog Born and still lives in Cardiff, where he runs the Stationery Office Oriel Bookshop in association with the Arts Council of Wales. He is a poet, short-fiction writer, editor and literary innovator. Turning early to poetry because he couldn't sing, Peter Finch has developed into a leading literary performer on the UK circuit. He has published more than 20 poetry titles, a collection of short fiction and a number of successful guides to the publishing process.

Credits include poetry collections, *Useful* (his latest) and *Poems for Ghosts* (Seren); and non-fiction books, *How to Publish Yourself* (Allison & Busby) and *The Poetry Business* (Seren).

Examples of his verse and his visual work appear on his web site at http://dialspace.dial.pipex.com/peter.finch/.

Question What are your views on the pros and cons of self-publishing?

I self-published my first book, a pamphlet of poems entitled *Wanted For Writing Poetry* co-authored with Stephen Morris. We had a Wanted poster for the cover which made us look like Wild West gunmen. Production was simple, cheap and easy. The book went by the fistful at readings. I've been fascinated by the process of doing it yourself ever since (see *How To Publish Yourself*, Allison & Busby). My second book, *Pieces of the Universe* came out the same way, as did *Blats*, my surrealist, experimental novel. They were exciting times.

At bottom, self-publishing involves the author in the adrenalin-pumping risk of publishing, in a way that having your title out from a trade publisher never can. Self-publishers by definition need to be pushy self-promoters forever mentioning their latest book and then producing copies from their bags. Corner someone and then don't let them go until they've bought. If you can't manage that, then my advice is not to bother. Self-publishing is as much about marketing and promotion as it is about dealing with print and design. Writing comes a slow, poor third.

Certainly, given the choice between a trade edition and one I'd done myself, I'd go for the professional. Individuals rarely have the resources of full-time publishers and although the control and speed of production that DIY brings can be addictive, it is in the area of distribution that most individuals fall down. Not that it isn't possible: witness the examples of best-selling authors Timothy Mo and Jill Paton Walsh. You self-publish, usually, because at the time there appears to be no other way of getting the thing out. Aeron Clement did that with his badger novel *Cold Moons*. Sold it over the counter at his local pub. Then Penguin came along and bought the rights. Wham! Success CAN happen.

Before starting down the self-publishing route, do study what is by far and away the best book on the subject – Peter Finch's *How to Publish Yourself* (Allison & Busby). Peter KNOWS – he has self-published, been published commercially and has sold the results of both.

Be careful not to confuse self-publishing with vanity publishing. There can be no doubt, if you self-publish, you make all the decisions, do all the work, reap all the hoped-for dividends. A vanity publisher is easy to spot:

● They advertise for authors ('real' publishers are inundated with book offers – they need never ask for more);
● They INEVITABLY say that your work is good and worthy of publication;
● They ask for vast sums of money 'towards the cost of publication';
● They present you with a voluminous contract, promising over-large royalties and other unfulfillable rewards.

Run from them. Far better, self-publish – there are fewer sharks in that water. But above all ... be business-like.

APPENDIX 1

GLOSSARY OF WRITING BUSINESS TERMS

Advance The payment to an author, of anticipated future royalties relating to a book not yet, or just, published. The important point is that an advance is ... an advance against future earnings and has to be 'earned out' before further royalty payments become due. An advance may be paid in several parts – any or all of the following: on signature of the Agreement, on delivery of the manuscript and on publication of the book. If royalties on sales do not 'earn out' the advance, it is not repayable to the publisher.

If a publisher cancels a book, through no fault of the author, after an Agreement has been signed but before publication, advances already paid are not (usually) repayable to the publisher – and unpaid parts of the advance may still be payable. Negotiate.

Agreement The form of contract between an author and a publisher in respect of one or more books. (For detailed analysis, see pp 95-103.)

aka An acronym for *also known as* – a way of indicating an author's pen-name.

ASCII file The initials are the acronym for American Standard Code for Information Interchange, and are pronounced *ass-key*. Virtually all word processors will convert one of their own documents into an ASCII file – a text-only file omitting format, etc., – which can be read by any other computer. (An ASCII file is sometimes referred to, in computer terminology, as a text-only or DOS file.) Increasingly, publishers welcome an ASCII file of a book manuscript – in addition to the conventional typescript.

Copyright The ownership of the right to copy a writer's work. Copyright of written work is automatically vested in the writer as soon as it is committed to paper (or electronic record) and is the writer's property until 70 years after his/her demise (*see* Chapter 7).

Desk-top publishing (DTP) Not what it says it is. Basically, a computer program which enables the skilful user to prepare material in the form of a book (or leaflet) page. This is little more than a typesetting job – a small part of the full publishing process. The layout of text on a book page is a skilled job: few writers will be competent to take on this task, but some wannabes may think that they are (*see* Chapter 8 for comments and advice on self-publishing).

Edition Copies of a book printed at one time – or several times without significant text changes – and similarly bound. Thus, a book may have two identical but separate hardback and paperback editions; there can, however, be several reprints or print runs within a single edition. (A print run is the number of copies printed at any one time.) Once the text is significantly changed, the book becomes a revised edition. (A new ISBN – see below – is used for each edition, but not for reprints or further print runs.)

Editor The editor of a magazine is in overall charge of the magazine's content: he/she may be assisted by other editors dealing with fiction and features – and possibly by other editorial 'departments'. A magazine's sub-editor has a similar role to a publisher's copy editor, see below.

In a publishing office there are two basic editorial functions which are sometimes undertaken by the same person.

- **A commissioning editor** is usually the person who will *initiate* approval of a book project, whether author- or publisher-conceived. (Final acceptance is usually a joint – editorial, sales, management – decision with the report on the book being presented by the commissioning editor.) Having identified, in-house, a potential niche/market for a book, a commissioning editor may sometimes go out looking for someone to write it – and then commission it.

- **A copy editor** (sometimes called a line editor) will go carefully through the accepted book text – line by line – checking consistency and accuracy of punctuation, spelling and grammar; checking understanding (if the copy editor can't understand what the author is driving at, neither will the general reader), and anomalies (such as name-changes, eye-colour changes, etc.). Usually, the copy editor will check corrections with the author.

FBSR The standard abbreviation of First British Serial Rights – which 'translates' to the right to publish for the first time in Britain in a magazine (i.e. serial, as opposed to book, publication).

Invoice A bill for work done/delivered. (See example on page 36.)

ISBN (International Standard Book Number) A unique 10-digit reference number identifying every published book, its geographical area of origin and its publisher. Thus: this book's ISBN (see back cover and page iv in the prelims) – and its meaning – is:

0	–	7490	–	0362	–	6
English-speaking Country		Allison & Busby		*The Business of Writing*		A check digit

List, publisher's A publisher's list is his catalogue of published books. The back list consists of books published previously, prior to the current season, which remain in print and available for sale.

Literary agent A person who acts on behalf of an author, finding *the right* publisher and negotiating financial terms. A literary agent often provides a 'shoulder to cry on' for the author in difficulties – 'blocked', in need of work, etc. A literary agent often has much editorial experience gained in a publisher's office, and good contacts with publishers. A literary agent is expected to be aware of up-to-date trends in the publishing world – and the current needs of specific publishers. Some agents offer editorial advice or services to their authors. An agent makes his/her living by levying a percentage (usually 10 to 15 per cent) on all the writing earnings of each agented author.

Outline A brief statement of the content of a proposed feature article. An outline should also include 'the hook' – the title and opening paragraph(s). An outline is submitted to a magazine editor in the hope of a go-ahead. An outline is sometimes incorporated within a query letter (*see* Figure 4.1, p 63).

PLR (Public Lending Right A scheme whereby each time a (PLR-registered) book is borrowed from a UK public library, the author is paid a small sum, annually, in arrears. (For more details see Chapter 6 p 87.)

Proofs A preliminary print of a typeset manuscript, sent to the author for checking and correction of typographical and layout errors. Today, usually in the form of finished book pages with the text more-or-less centred on A4 sheets. (In days gone by, long sheets of *galley proofs* were sent for checking before being cut-and-pasted into pages. Computerisation makes this preliminary stage unnecessary except, possibly, for complicated academic texts – with formulae, etc.) Will include run-of-text illustrations or blank spaces where possibly incomplete illustrations are to be inserted. And remember: PROOFS ARE FOR CORRECTION, *NOT* FOR SECOND THOUGHTS. Authors' mind-changes can prove expensive ... for the author. You WILL be billed.

Publisher An individual or company that publishes books as a commercial operation. The publisher takes the commercial risk of accepting an author's work, agreeing to pay for it, preparing (editing, etc.) and paying for it to be made into a book, and marketing it. Publishing was once an 'occupation for gentlemen' – nowadays, it has to be profitable, or go to the wall.

Royalty The payment to an author of a percentage of, conventionally, the retail price of the book made in respect of each sale. 'Industry standard' royalty rates are: hardback, 10 per cent; paperback 7.5 per cent – on the first block of sales. Royalty rates on mass market paperback sales are often at a lower percentage than the 7.5 per cent which is currently paid on trade paperbacks. Individual Agreements may provide for the royalty rates to increase once a specified sales figure is reached.

Some publishers prefer – supposedly for ease of accounting – royalties based on a percentage of their net receipts from book sales. (For instance, if ten copies of a £10-list-price book are sold to a bookseller at 50 per cent discount, the publisher receives £50 and the author a percentage of that figure.) Clearly, a royalty based on net receipts has to be at a higher percentage than one based on the retail price – and with discounts frequently in the 50 to 60 per cent region, at least double the 'standard' retail price rate is appropriate.

SAE A stamped, (self-)addressed envelope – which should always be provided when submitting unsolicited work or queries to a magazine or publisher. The SAE should always be of an appropriate size – and sufficiently stamped – for the return of the submitted material. Failure to provide an SAE may result in the submission being binned, unlooked at. In America the conventional term is SASE – a self-addressed stamped envelope.

Slush pile The uncomplimentary – but largely justified – name give to the often vast quantity of unsolicited material continually delivered to magazine and publishing offices. Consideration of the slush pile has to take second (or third) place to consideration of commissioned or agented work, or submissions from known writers, arriving in the offices. The slush pile IS looked at, eventually, and items therein are sometimes accepted.

Synopsis A much-condensed outline of a proposed work. For works of fiction, the synopsis should be conventional text – i.e. a readable condensation of the plot and introducing the characters – rather than a list of headings, and should NOT omit the final 'punch-line'. (Publishers will neither steal this nor disclose it to others – but they must be told it.) For non-fiction works the synopsis is more usually a list of understandable note-like headings.

Trade paperback A paperback edition often slightly 'up-market' of a mass-market paperback – better quality paper, better binding, etc., often slightly larger page-size – of a book which is not expected to sell in mass-market quantities.

APPENDIX 2

WRITERS' ORGANISATIONS

There are many advantages in belonging to a relevant writers' organisation. Some are trade unions, offering strength in numbers; others offer the ability to 'network' (to make contacts); others offer professional advice. Certainly it is worth any business-like writer joining one or more of the associations listed below. If nothing else, you will have the opportunity to meet others in the same trade, experiencing the same problems.

Professional associations – authors

The Society of Authors
An independent trade union, not affiliated to the Trades Union Congress, the Society has over 5,000 members. It caters for the needs of both fiction and non-fiction authors – it is geared mainly to those working in the world of books (*cf* The Writers' Guild, which is geared more to screenwriters). There are various specialist groups within the Society, e.g. for educational writers, scientific writers, children's writers, etc. It produces an excellent quarterly journal, *The Author* and several useful leaflets – the *Quick Guides* – all free to members. It has a small but efficient professional staff who will offer legal and general advice and guidance on all manner of authorial matters. The annual subscription is currently £70 (£65 by direct debit).

Further information from The Society of Authors, 84 Drayton Gardens, London SW10 9SB. Tel: 0171-373 6642.

The Writers' Guild of Great Britain
A TUC-affiliated but non-political trade union founded in 1959, the Guild was initially restricted to screen writers. In 1974 book authors and stage dramatists became eligible for membership. The Guild produces two newsletters for its members: one contains information 'From the Office'; the other, a quarterly, carries articles, letters, etc. from members. The Guild's annual membership fees are currently £70 plus one per cent of the member's earnings from professional writing in the previous calendar year.

Further information from The Writers' Guild of Great Britain, 430 Edgware Road, London W2 1EH. Tel: 0171-723 8074.

Professional associations – journalists

The National Union of Journalists
The trade union for journalists working in newspaper and magazine publishing. There is a specific section of the union for freelance journalists. Membership identifies you as a real professional and is always worth mentioning. The NUJ publishes *The Journalist*, *The Freelance Directory* and *The Freelance Fees Guide*.

Further information from The National Union of Journalists, Acorn House, 314 Gray's Inn Road, London WC1X 8DP. Tel: 0171-278 7916.

Other useful organisations

The Crime Writers' Association
For professional writers of crime novels, etc. Publishes a monthly magazine *Red Herrings*.

Further information from the secretary, Judith Cutler at 60 Drayton Road, Kings Heath, Birmingham B14 7LR.

The Romantic Novelists' Association (RNA)
The purpose of the RNA is to raise the prestige of romantic

authorship. It is open to romantic and historical novelists – it offers help and guidance to unpublished romantic novelists.

Further information from the chairman, Angela Arney at 43 Wilton Gardens, Shirley, Southampton SO1 2QS.

The Society of Women Writers and Journalists (SWWJ)
The SWWJ holds monthly meetings/lectures and publishes *The Woman Journalist*.

Further information from the secretary, Jean Hawkes at 110 Whitehall Road, Chingford, London E4 6DW. Tel: 0181-529 0886.

The Women Writers Network
Founded in 1985, in London, the Women Writers Network provides a forum for the exchange of information, support and networking opportunities exclusively for women writers of all disciplines. The network holds monthly meetings in London and publishes a newsletter and members directory. The network is spreading to out-of-London members too. Annual subscription is currently £30.

Further information from Susan Kerr at 55 Burlington Lane, London W4 3ET. Tel: 0181-994 0598.

The Author-Publisher Network
The Author-Publisher Network is an association of writers who publish their own work – a source of information, ideas and encouragement. If you are contemplating self-publishing, you should join them. Annual subscription is £25.

Further information from the chairman, Clive Brown at 26 Ladymeade, Ilminster, Somerset TA19 0EA. Tel: 01460-57314 (evenings).

APPENDIX 3

PROFESSIONAL ADVICE FOR BEGINNING WRITERS

Although I have made it clear, from the start of this book, that it is not about *how to write*, but about *how to be a business-like writer*, this appendix contains business-like writing advice for beginners – from the professionals who have provided their helpful comments throughout the earlier pages. When I circulated my list of business-type questions, I also asked if they had any general advice. Most made helpful suggestions ... Nearly all have the same attitude.

Anne Ashurst
Write every day. Don't ask family or friends for criticism unless you come from a long line of editors or agents. Make sure that your material suits the market it's intended for. Don't waste weeks/months on your first page, or chapter, trying to make it perfect, or you may lose impetus. Get the whole piece finished, and the experience you gain will show you how the beginning will work best. Keep up with contemporary trends, even if you don't approve of them. Finally, read, read, and read again.

Jo Bannister
Anyone contemplating writing must first do so as a hobby, something they enjoy doing for themselves. To decide you're going to be a professional author is like deciding you'll be a big-time show-jumper – for every one who makes money at it there are a thousand who spend money doing it. If you turn out to be particularly good, sooner or later someone may offer to pay you. But if they don't, it's only been a waste of time if you haven't

enjoyed it. So write for yourself first, potential buyers second. If you're good enough to make a business of this you probably enjoy writing what people enjoy reading anyway.

Simon Brett
Everything you write can be improved by cutting. Leave the manuscript for a month, then have another look at it, and it's amazing how many of your favourite bits will have become unnecessary.

Once you've got a project off your desk, forget about it and get on with the next thing. Then, if the original project is rejected, you can comfort yourself that you've 'moved on as a writer'.

Peter Finch
To write you have to write. This may sound obvious but it is amazing the number of people out there who claim to be writers but who actually turn out very little. Writers improve by keeping on. Don't scratch a few words for half an hour and then watch TV. Work for longer stretches – several hours concentrated, uninterrupted graft. As times passes your sentences will become more assured. And to write well you have to read. Do not be afraid of stealing other people's styles, images and ideas. It is the way the whole business is structured: you don't imagine that Shakespeare was the first to think up the plot for *Romeo and Juliet*, do you? Read vociferously, and not just the kind of material you know you like. Read widely, trawl the magazines, the journals, the anthologies. Keep your head down and eventually you'll find your own voice.

And perhaps most importantly, don't imagine that because you write you are unique. You are not. Writing is a very competitive field. What opportunities for success there are will be clamoured after. Drop pretension. So long as you believe in yourself and are willing to take the knocks and keep at it, then all will be fine.

Susan Moody
Don't give up. Read, read, read; write, write, write. Enjoy what you do because if you don't, why should the reader?

Pamela Oldfield
If you want to earn a good living from your work, write to please your readers, not to please yourself.

Diana Pullein-Thompson
Write from the heart; write about what you know; decide at the beginning the sort of reader you have in mind. Develop an ear for dialogue by listening to others' conversation – bus journeys are good for this – and become an observer rather than a talker. Read well-written books before starting your own work, but hold back while you are writing or you may, inadvertently, steal their style. It is often easier to find a publisher if you try to contribute to an established series, especially with children's books where single stories with no follow-ups are sometimes hard to sell. If at the end of two hours' work you don't feel drained, you are not putting enough effort and emotion into your writing.

Jean Saunders
Be as professional as you can. Writing is very competitive, and editors can pick and choose from any number of manuscripts that arrive on their desks daily. So good presentation and spelling counts, as does market study of the genre in which you want to write. Attend courses and lectures, read the relevant 'How-to' books, and take on board all the advice that applies to you – and then write your own book with your own voice.

Finally, have a story to tell and plan it well. It's surprising how many would-be novelists don't. Working out a skeleton plan of a novel takes time, but it's time well spent. It also irons out all the inconsistencies that can crop up if you rush blindly into writing your book with no forward planning. There are undoubtedly authors who can and do work very successfully this way, but for a beginner, my advice is to know where you're going, and to work out the route your characters will take to reach the end. Otherwise, it can be like boarding a train without knowing your destination.

Stella Whitelaw
Don't stop writing, don't give up. Don't send out inferior work just because your friend thinks it's wonderful. Be honest with yourself; be your own sternest critic. Discipline yourself with rules and deadlines, for instance:

- I will write 1,000 words a day.
- I will submit four short stories a month.
- I will finish this book by Christmas.

INDEX

INDEX

Other Allison & Busby Writers' Guides

A Selection from Allison & Busby's Writers' Guides Series

Please send me
(tick here)

☐	0 7490 0203 4	How to Write Five-Minute Features	Alison Chisholm
☐	0 7490 0289 1	The Craft of Writing Poetry	Alison Chisholm
☐	0 7490 0294 8	A Practical Poetry Course	Alison Chisholm
☐	0 7490 0311 1	The Craft of Novel-Writing	Dianne Doubtfire
☐	0 7490 0301 4	How to Publish Yourself	Peter Finch
☐	0 7490 0391 X	How to Publish Your Poetry	Peter Finch
☐	0 7490 0197 6	How to Write a Blockbuster	Sarah Harrison
☐	0 7490 0258 1	How to Write for Children	Tessa Krailing
☐	0 7490 0192 5	How to Write Realistic Dialogue	Jean Saunders
☐	0 7490 0249 2	How to Compile Crosswords	Graham Stevenson
☐	0 7490 0298 0	The Craft of Writing Articles	Gordon Wells
☐	0 7490 0229 8	The Magazine Writer's Handbook	Gordon Wells
☐	0 7490 0209 3	How to Write Short-Short Stories	Stella Whitelaw
☐	0 7490 0345 6	The Crime Writer's Handbook	Douglas Wynn

ALLISON & BUSBY WRITERS' GUIDES ARE £8.99 EACH. THEY ARE AVAILABLE FROM YOUR LOCAL BOOKSHOP, THROUGH OUR WEBSITE (www.allisonandbusby.ltd.uk) OR BY MAIL ORDER

To order please send a cheque or Postal Order (UK sterling only) payable to Allison & Busby Ltd. Please add 75 pence per book for postage and packing in the UK. Overseas customers should add £1 per book for postage and packing.

NAME: _____

ADDRESS: _____

_____

_____

☐   Please tick box if you wish to receive our latest catalogue and stocklist.

Send your orders to:
Allison & Busby Ltd
Writers' Guides
114 New Cavendish Street
London
W1M 7FD

All orders will be despatched immediately, but please allow 14 days for delivery in UK, 28 days worldwide.